T0123325

BEING ON THE INSIDE - THE CHURCH IN MOTION

Empowering Your Today for a
Better Tomorrow

LEONIE WALTERS

authorHOUSE®

AuthorHouse™
1663 Liberty Drive
Bloomington, IN 47403
www.authorhouse.com
Phone: 833-262-8899

Published by AuthorHouse 10/22/2021

ISBN: 978-1-6655-3151-1 (sc)
ISBN: 978-1-6655-3149-8 (hc)
ISBN: 978-1-6655-3150-4 (e)

Library of Congress Control Number: 2021913886

Print information available on the last page.

CONTENTS

ACKNOWLEDGEMENTS

O give thanks unto the Lord; for he is good: for his mercy endureth forever (Psalm 136:1). I want to thank God for his grace and mercy for instructing me to write this book, without him the completion of this book would have been impossible. To Mikyle (son) and Shikyla (daughter) who are always by my side, encouraging me to complete this assignment. To my sisters Toya, and Pamella who prayed me through, and holding me up in prayers along the way. Thank you all!

In the book of Matthew 16:18 Jesus said to Peter,".......That thou art Peter, and upon this rock I will build my church; and the gates of hell shall not prevail against it." We are the church up on the revelation knowledge of Christ Jesus, we are being built in a spiritual house. The God that we serve is not learnt, he is revealed unto us and the gates of hell shall not prevail against it. Jesus said, I give unto you, the keys of the kingdom of heaven: and whatsoever thou shalt bind on earth shall be bound in heaven: and whatsoever thou shalt loose on earth shall be loose in heaven. How can we bind and loose if we do not know our purpose and who we are in God. We must be able to position ourselves in God! When a police officer walks up to a person, he or she identifies his or herself with a badge. When they are able to identify themselves, they show authority over that environment. Knowing who you are in God will give you the power over the enemy. Elijah stood on the top of Mount Carmel against eight hundred and fifty of Baal's Prophet, he was one man, yet he knew who he was and to whom he belong. His experience and relationship with God gave him the confidence to stand knowing it's not him, but it's a supernatural force that is in operation. We serve a supernatural God, a God that can do all things. He is also a God of order.

As believers we have to seek him to find out his purpose and assignment for our lives. Our purpose will become clear when we find ourselves in the proper place where we can line up with the words of Almighty God. There are so many believers in the body of Christ that have been misplaced and mishandled by others. There are many dedicated Christians in the church who are not in their proper position or location, they are in violation of the kingdom of God. According to Ephesians 4:11, God has called his people into various offices, operating in the fivefold ministries for the perfecting of the saints, for the work of the ministry, for the edifying of the body of Christ. When we as the body of Christ come into the knowledge of his purpose for our lives, the church will be in order. There are so many self-appointed believers in the church today. Some people believe that if you don't have a title in front of your name, you are not important in the church. There are also leaders who appoint certain members to preform roles and responsibilities in the church because of their status, occupation, and education. These members have been misplaced, they are appointed by man and not by God according to his plan. When a person is placed in the wrong position in the church, it can give access to open doors for the enemy to enter. When there is a war, soldiers with special training are sent out and placed at the frontline while some are in reserve. We as a body in Christ need to be strategic in what we do or think. Some people in the church are in position because of favoritism, or the amount of money they are putting in the offering basket, or in some cases the way they look physically and the clothes they wear. This is wrong and needs to be addressed. We need to rely on the Holy Spirit in every area of the ministry to reveal our individual assignment in the church. We are having an identity crisis in the body of Christ! It is best for leaders to ask God for instruction when they are assigning roles and responsibilities, or giving titles to individual in their congregation. Leaders have a lot of responsibilities concerning their ministry and those who they choose to work in certain positions. God has given them the grace for leadership.

There are also believers that have been sitting in church for years, not knowing their purpose or their assignment. Some are stagnant, some are intimidated, some are paralyzed by fear, some are just being disobedient, and some say that they have been waiting on God for many years. Believers are still waiting for God to take them out of the benches and place them in position in the churches. But, can I tell you that, there are times when God will put us through the process and get some things on the inside of us. Sometimes he wants to pull something out of us. We cannot remain stagnant! Growth must take place. I pray you are not in your waiting period when God is saying move. I pray that you will not be too busy to hear him when he is speaking to you. God is waiting on you to ask him to show you your purpose yet, you are waiting on him to lead you into your purpose. You have an individual responsibility to seek God concerning your purpose and assignment. Sometimes your assignment will look impossible but God is the one that will give you the enablement to do it. Ask Him! He will respond to you when you ask. God is the one that gives you the anointing to carry out the tasks that he has for you to do. You may be gifted but it is the anointing that will make the difference in whatever you do for God. It is the anointing that will break the yoke and set the captives free! It will enable you to press beyond your human ability, the things that seems difficult to the ordinary people will be done with ease. I ask you this question," What has God called you to do and what is your assignment?" I want you to seek God, find the your answer, then put it in the blank space below;

My Assignment is: ....

You would be surprise to know who you really are in God and who he has called you to be. You would be amazed to find out who is the real you!

Now there are so many wonderful and dedicated men and women of God, and there are some leaders out there who constantly stay connected to the vine which is in Christ Jesus. They know that it is not their will but God's will that has to be done. They totally rely on the Holy Spirit and his instruction and do it God's way. They rely on the Holy Spirit to reveal the purpose and plan for the people, each and every step of the way. May God bless them for their sacrificial offering as they present their body as a vessel that is worthy to be used for service. Our reward is in heaven, we must work the works of him that sent us, while it is day: because the night cometh, when no man can work.

I pray by the authority of Jesus Christ, the son of God that you will rise and take your proper place with the leading of the Holy Spirit and leadership in the church. No one can truly be successful without the grace of God. We are totally dependent on him, God has already given you the grace to sustain you. Amen!

Philippians 2:13 for it is God which worketh in you both to will and to do of his good pleasure.

God did not anoint you to sit on the anointing and do nothing. The anointing is not for you, it is to do his will, amen. There is a time and a season for everything on the face of the earth. You have to seek God to know if it is your season to go forth with your leaders' permission. When it is the right time, God will also thrust you forth. There is a time when you have to sit also, and wait for him because there are stuff that he needs to take out, work out, or put in you. Some people needs healing and deliverance. Some people may be struggling with drug addiction, bitterness, un-forgiveness, spirit of rejection, sexual addiction, sexual abuse, physical abuse, alcoholism, as well as other spirits that often wrestle against us. There are so many more strongholds, and even when we are at a good place, some of us still struggle with these things. God wants us to be whole so we can be more effective in the body of Christ. If you have been struggling with any of these, I want to pray for you but you have to believe in order to receive your deliverance. Praying and submission to God is the gateway to overcome any obstacles and hindrances.

I decree and declare by the authority of Jesus Christ you are healed and set free from every spirit that is contrary to the spirit of God! I pray that you will come into his purpose and calling in name of Jesus Christ. I pray that every chains and whatsoever that is holding you bound will be broken in the name of Jesus. I pray that you will press your way through like the woman who had the issue of blood for twelve years but when she heard that Jesus was passing by, she pressed her way through the crowd. Jesus is passing your way today! Hold on to him and let him restore you! Let God have his way in you and through you in the name of Jesus, Amen.

The Bible says in the book of St Luke 4:18 that, Jesus came to heal the broken hearted, to preach deliverance to the captives, and recovering of sight to the blind, to set at liberty them that are bruised. Claim your victory in the name of Jesus, the one who is our mediator between God and man; Amen. As children of God, we have the right to speak things into existence and it shall come to pass. Jesus Christ paid it all at Calvary. To God be the glory for the things he has done, and the things he is about to do in your life! *For he knows the thoughts that he thinks toward us; the thoughts that will bring peace, and not evil! These thoughts will give us an expected end.* This is the original plan that God has for us, amen.

THE NECESSITY OF THE FIVEFOLD MINISTRY

The fivefold ministry is just a starting point for understanding our divine DNA and destiny. This ministry is not something we volunteer for, such as ushering, worship, charity, or fellowship, but these roles are appointed by God. *So Christ himself gave the apostles, the prophets, the evangelists, the pastors and teachers, to equip his people for works of service, so that the body of Christ may be built up until we all reach unity in the faith and in the knowledge of the Son of God and become mature, attaining to the whole measure of the fullness of Christ.* (Ephesians 4:11-13). The purpose of fivefold ministry, then, is not to wave a title around or travel from church to church receiving praises and honorariums. The purpose of fivefold ministry is to "equip God's people for works of service…" The only way to equip someone for something is to be a living example of it. You cannot equip a person to serve unless you yourself are a better servant than they are. As Jesus said, "Anyone who wants to be first must be the very last, and the servant of all." (See Mark 9:35.)

The fivefold ministry is needed in the 'house of God' because his house needs to be in order for the power of God to move mightily. In the book of 2 Chronicles 7, the Bible says that Solomon build the temple and every one was in their proper place. And, the glory of the God came down in the temple. As children of God, we are like soldiers in the army of the God. As compared to the armed forces, soldiers are ranked and placed in positions according to their work, behavior, capabilities, experience and the years they have been serving. In other words, they are not ranked based on how they dress or how they look. As soldiers in the army of the Lord we have to put on the whole armor of the Almighty God. Ephesians 6:11 says' "Put on the whole armor of God, that you may be able to stand against the wiles of the devil".

I speak to your spirit to rise. I declare a shift in your spirit! Shake off depression and low self-esteem in the name of Jesus! Come forth Lazarus, shed your grave clothes and step into your purpose in the name of Jesus! Now rejoice in Jesus name! Hallelujah. For the kingdom of God suffer violence and you need to take it by force. Rise and walk in Jesus name! I speak to your mind to be loose from solitary confinement, lift your hands and praise him, hallelujah! Every spirit of hindrance has to go in the name of Jesus Christ. You are a man or a woman of purpose, stand with your loins girt with truth. Many are the afflicted of the righteous, but God deliver them (**not some but**) all. Jesus said, "come unto me all that are heavy laden and I will give you rest". God is no respecter of person. If he did it for me, he can do it for you.

RANKS

As believers in the body of Christ, we are not to be caught up with just having a title but to do the will of God our father. God is the one that gives 'true' promotion and titles. There is a trend sweeping in the churches today, it is the season for titles. Titles have become give-a-ways and deals, if you want it just catch it! The most common rank in the fivefold ministry is the prophet; everyone wants to be a prophet. A prophet is God's mouth piece on the earth. They are chosen by God not man. You can choose to be a doctor or nurse but you cannot choose to be a prophet, it is *'not up for grabs'* it is given by God. He said to Jeremiah, *before I formed thee in the belly I knew thee; and before thou camest forth out of the womb I sanctified thee, and I ordained thee a prophet unto the nations.* There are self-appointed prophets as well. They are the ones who stand before Yahweh's people and 'pro-**phe-lies'** (tell them lies). Be vigilant children of God, try the spirit by the spirit, and let no man deceive you.

Matthew 24:11 speaks about the false prophets that shall rise, and shall deceive many. Children of God watch, stay in your watch-towers. Matthew 24 states, "For there shall arise false prophets, and shall shew great signs and wonders; in so much that, if it were possible, they shall deceive the very elect". A perfect example is in Exodus when God send Moses to tell Pharaoh to let his people go. When Moses went, he did what God told him to do. He threw down his rod and it became a serpent and Pharaoh called his wise men and sorcerers, and the magicians of Egypt; and their rods also became snakes. There is always a counterfeit for every real. The enemy is a deceiver but God is always ahead of him. Where are the evangelist, teachers and pastors? Get into your position! Jehovah is the one that ranks you in the spirit. We all have different assignments in the spiritual realms and we have authority over different realm of the spirit. On the Mount of Transfiguration, Jesus said to Peter, *"And I will give unto thee the keys of the kingdom of heaven: and whatsoever thou shalt bind on earth shall be bound in heaven: and whatsoever thou shalt loose on earth shall be loose in heaven"* (**Matthew 16-19**). He gave Peter access to bind whatever needs to be bound and to loose that which has been bound.

Our individual calling is different from each other. Christ did not call us all to be Apostles or Evangelist. Each of those whom he called, has received different spiritual gifts and therefore has different assignment to do. An Apostle will not operate at the same level or hierarchy as a teacher, neither does he carry the same anointing. When we are able to recognize our rightful place in God, and seek to align our daily life with his word, we can do exploit in the kingdom of God. We will become a threat to the kingdom of darkness when we are able to fully recognize who we are, and STAND armored in the face of our adversary. Since God has also given us the authority to bind and loose, we must exercise the power to do so in humility and obedience.

We are many members but one body in Christ. For example, your body is a whole. If your hands are cut off you will not function effectively in the capacity that you should because your body works as a physical whole. This is the same for the spiritual man, in the body of Christ we all need each other to function in a holistic way, the local members of the church needs the leaders and the leaders need the members.

The Apostle work with the prophets, the prophet work with the evangelists, the evangelists work alongside the pastors, the pastor work along with the teachers, and the musician and the singers work together. Music plays a very important role in the church. Playing musical instruments in itself is a ministry. Musicians cannot only play in the church because they have gifted hands or skills and talents, but they have to be called into that ministry. They need to constantly be in prayer and fasting (consecration) in order to be effective in the church. There is a certain sound for each time we go before the Almighty God in worship. The worship leader should be able to discern the atmosphere and sing a song for that moment. I have seen so many instances where the Spirit of God is moving and the worship leader was not in sync or able to discern the shift in the atmosphere. Discernment will allow the worship leader to stop that song, grab the flow and start that "at-the-moment song" that will instantaneously make the connection with the atmospheric shift. This is why it is so important for believers to be in their proper place and assignment and have 'spiritual eyes and ears' to discern what's is happening around them.

1 Samuel 16:23 mentioned that, when the evil spirit from God was upon Saul, David took a harp, and played with his hand. This musical prelude was refreshing to the soul of Saul

as well as causing the evil spirit to depart from him. In Acts Chapter 2 the Bible says that, on the day of Pentecost they were on one accord in one place and suddenly there came a sound from heaven as of a rushing mighty wind, and it filled the entire house where they were sitting. Children of God, seek him to find out his purpose and calling for your life! Some believers spend more time in church trying to tear down each other than to help someone find their way or walk in Jehovah's purpose for their life. When I just got saved, it was a struggle for me. I did not have the support I needed, instead of support I was been ridiculed and ostracized. We must be careful about how we treat the new believers in the church.

There are church members who focus on being carnal minded, full of strife, and envy. Sometimes it is so discouraging to new believers because no one encourages, nurture or mentor them. Let us come together in unity, let us support each other, for we wrestle not against flesh and blood but against principalities and powers, against the rulers of darkest and spiritual wickedness in high places. Let us love each other, John 15:12 says "this is my commandment, that ye love one another as I have loved you." Matthew 12:25 says "every kingdom divided against itself is brought to desolation; and every city or house divided against itself shall not stand". I pray in the name of Jesus Christ that as you read this book, you will be empowered in the gift or gifts that God has given you and the work that he has called you to do in the name of Jesus. If you are a young believer be encouraged; be strong, be empowered for the journey in the name of Jesus.

In 2 Timothy 4:5 (MSG version), the Bible admonished us to keep our eyes on what we are doing and accept the hard times along with the good. We must keep the message alive and do a thorough job as God's servant. *"But watch thou in all things, endure afflictions, do the work of an evangelist, make full proof of thy ministry".* (2 Timothy 4:5 KJV)

Whereas, in Romans 6:23, the Bible says" *for the wages of sin is death; but the gift of God is eternal life through Jesus Christ our Lord".*

Whether you are called to be a preacher, or a teacher, an evangelist, or a singer, a steward or a servant to clean the church, God got you! The strength of all ministries depend on having a dedicated and personal relationship with the Almighty God. Your strength in God depends on having a lifestyle that is rooted and grounded in prayer and supplication unto God. You have to recognize that it is he who equips you with your gift or gifts and anoints you to fulfill his purpose. Rejoice for the step of a righteous man are ordered by the Almighty God. In Matt 16:24-25, Jesus said to his disciples *if any man will come after me, let him deny himself, and take up his cross, and follow me. For whosoever will save his life shall lose it: and whosoever will lose his life for my sake shall find it.*

To maintain your anointing it takes great sacrifice! There are so many great men and women of God who sacrificed their time in studying the word and in constant prayer and fasting, seeking the face of God for instruction to pour into their life. For some of us, it is the earnest cries of intercessors that help to put us where we are today. We thank God for the earthen vessels that he used to pour into us and to declare his Word concerning our lives. Yes!!!! Jesus paid the price at the cross but we have to physically and spiritually lay prostrate at the altar and stay there. We need not to be covetous or hateful towards any one especially if God is using them as his oracle, or because of the anointing upon their life. The anointing does not happen overnight, but comes through pressing, pushing, pain, suffering, sorrows, prayer and travailing, fasting, and a hunger and thirst for the things of God. If you have not seen the sacrifice that the true servants have made, then you have no right to judge them or be skeptical of their gifts and anointing. Pray for them that God will continue to sustain them! Pray that God will help you to live a consecrated life so that he can use you as his chosen vessel.

1 Thessalonians 5:17 pray without ceasing. You need to pray for your leaders because the devil is like a roaring lion seeking who he may devour and he always goes for the head first. Pray constantly for each and every one of them in Jesus name that he will continue to strengthen them, and that they may walk circumspectly according to the Word of God in their calling. I pray for a shield of fire around every leader and their families in

the name of Jesus. Father, I pray that you will place people around them that will be consistent in interceding on their behalf. I pray that their feet will not slip and they will not slumber nor sleep but they will press into what you have called them to do. Keep them Lord! Hide them in the shadow of you wings because your word must come to pass according Isaiah 55. Hallelujah! I pray that the ministry that you have entrusted in their hands will grow and strengthened. I pray that they will have the spirit of the sons of Issachar knowing the time and season in Jesus name, Amen.

SACRIFICE

Let not sin therefore reign in your mortal body, that ye should obey it in the lusts thereof. Neither yield ye your members as instruments of unrighteousness unto sin: but yield yourselves unto God as those that are alive from the dead, and your members as instruments of righteousness unto God. (Romans 6:12-13 KJV)

Romans 6:12-13 MSG says,' *That means you must not give sin a vote in the way you conduct your lives. Don't give it the time of day. Don't even run little errands that are connected with that old way of life. Throw yourself wholeheartedly and full-time----remember, you've been raised from the dead! – into God's way of doing things.*

These scripture teaches us that we are to yield ourselves to the Almighty God on a daily basis. God's desire for us is to present ourselves upon the altar as a living sacrifice, we are to shun sin or in other words, flee from sin. The scripture says resist the devil and he will flee, so I am encouraging us to flee from sin!

Romans 12:1-2 Paul states" I beseech you therefore, brethren, by the mercies of God that ye present your bodies a living sacrifice, holy, acceptable unto God, which is your reasonable service and be not conformed to this world; but be ye transformed by the renewing of your mind, that ye may prove what is that good, and acceptable, and perfect, will of God.

God desires that we sacrifice our time for his purpose (Ephesians 5:16; Colossians 4:5). God wants us to use our time wisely. All of our accomplishments are because of his hands in our lives today. Everything that we have is because of Jehovah Jireh our provider; things are given to us for us to give back to him.

In Philippians 4:18, Paul says that such a sacrifice is an odor of sweet smell, a sacrifice acceptable, well pleasing to God. Sacrifice your time! There are so many ways to sacrifice your time unto him; give a helping hand to the needy, feed the hungry, buy a bag of groceries for someone you know is struggling outside and the church. There are so many silent believers who are at their last and are afraid to say something because of shame, pride or they don't want to be the topic of careless and deceitful conversations. We have to be careful how we handle these delicate situations in the body of Christ.

Acts 20:35 tells us that Jesus says it is more blessed to give than to receive. We have to be our brother's keeper; Jesus Christ walked by the pool of Bethesda and found an impotent man who had been ill for thirty-eight years. An angel had troubled the water each year, but the man had been unable to reach the water before others in order to receive his healing. The man's helpless situation touched Jesus, and he healed him. We are to watch out for each other in that same manner. This impotent man had been in that same situation for thirty-eight years and no one paid attention to his need. There was no one to give him a hand! I heard a Pastor ministering some time ago and he said that the man was blaming his situation on others. Sometimes we quickly point our finger on someone else instead of taking responsibility for our situation, and then there are times when we need help. This man was physically ill, he was unable to get himself in the pool. He needed help in that situation! God wants us to be a blessing to others especially if we are in any position to help them. I pray in the name of Jesus Christ, that you will receive your healing if you are in a similar position like the man at the pool of Bethesda. It is not by might nor by power but by the spirit of the Almighty God.

Isaiah 53:5 says, "He was wounded for our transgressions, he was bruised for our iniquities: the chastisement of our peace was upon him; and with his stripes we are healed".

If you believe it shout," hallelujah" hallelujah" hallelujah" to the Lamb of God! Your faith has made you whole, give him the glory.

Every stripes that he took were for your healing, give him thanks, there's a song that says, "Give thanks with a grateful heart, give thanks to the Holy One give thanks for he has given Jesus Christ his son give thanks: and now let the weak says I am strong let the poor says I am rich because of what the Lord has done for us give thanks." Hallelujah! Just take a moment and give him thanks.

In 1 Thessalonians 5:18, Paul says in everything give thanks for this the will of God in Jesus Christ concerning you. Apart from humility and obedience, God responds to a thankful heart. Other ways of sacrificing your time is through prayer, fasting and reading the word of God. These are like vitamins that will strengthened your walk with the Almighty God. Prayer keeps you connected to the source, it propels you in the realm of the spirit, it strengthen the inner man, and keep you closer to God! Jesus says I am the vine, ye are the branches: He that abideth in me, and I in him, the same bringeth forth much fruit: for without me ye can do nothing," (**John 15:5**) Abiding in Christ is the only way to fruitfulness, friendship and answered prayer. Prayer is also a powerful weapon against the enemy. Any traps that the enemy has set up against you, your prayer can dismantle and destroy them. The word of God says life and death is in the power of the tongue.

Paul told the Thessalonians in Chapter 5:17 that they are to pray without ceasing. Therefore, we should never stop praying; pray until something happens, and even when it happens, pray and give him thanks. Jesus spoke a parable unto them to this end that men ought always to pray and not faint" (Luke 18:1). Prayer will change your situation and turn things around, prayer empowers your spiritual walk with God and bring you into right standing with Christ Jesus. It is the key to spiritual warfare. Prayer is a weapon, it thrust you into your destiny. I pray that Jesus Christ will give you the strength to go through whatever you are going through. With replenished strength, you shall COME OUT knowing that every situation is for the greater good in Jesus name. Rest assure that the Almighty God is with you in every situation. I am persuaded that God will see you through, I have no doubt that he is able to make a way for you! Put your trust in him, there is nothing impossible for the Almighty God. There is a daily cross that we all have to carry. He said, "Take up your cross and follow me." The Bible says in James 5:13, is any among you afflicted? Let him pray. Is any merry? Let him sing Psalms". There are times when we pray and we expect God to move immediately, but it is in Yahweh's timeframe and our best interest to delay the answers. It may not be the season and time for it or we are not at the place of maturity to receive what he has for us. Sometime we pray for the things that God don't not want us to have, we need to pray that his will be done in your life instead of what we want. Only God knows what is best for you, he will never put more on you than what you can bear.

The Apostle Paul mentioned in 1 Corinthians 10:13 that God is faithful enough to keep you during your temptations and that he will not suffer you to be tempted above that ye are able; but he will also make a way to escape, and that you may be able to bear it. Just remember that delay is not denial. The story of Lazarus is a typical example that delay is not denial. Sometimes the things we are praying for are not what God wants for us. He desires us to have the best. He is a Giver of Good Gifts! Be patient, God is not through with you yet! Hold on to his unchanging hands, he never fails. Jesus is the same yesterday today and forevermore, He is Jehovah-Shammah, he's always there. If you're in prison, he's your escape! Use his name, Jesus and continue to be steadfast and unmovable, always abound in Jesus Christ. This race is not for the swift but for those that can endure to the end.

11 Timothy 2:3 Paul says "Endure hardness, as a good soldier of Jesus Christ". So, endure as good solders in the army of the Almighty God. Keep your eyes on the one who hold your future in is hands Hallelujah" Hallelujah" Glory be to the Almighty God.

FASTING

We have to be consistent in prayer and fasting. So many believers tend to fast when they are at their lowest or only when there's a personal need for something from God. This should not be so, fasting is spiritual cleansing, it puts your flesh under subjection and empowers your spiritual walk with God. Fasting is a denial of one's self and presenting yourself in humility. You are hungry and thirsty after God, you yearn for the things of God, Your soul pants after God, like a deer that pants after the water brook. Fasting allows you to put yourself before Jesus Christ so that he can sift you and remove the dregs or debris, and refresh your soul with living waters. Fasting helps to provide spiritual detoxification of the body, it empowers your prayer to be more effective and shift you to a higher level in him. Fasting change things around you.

"Is not this the fast that I have chosen, to loose the bands of wickedness, to undo the heavy burdens, and to let the oppressed go free, and that ye break every yoke, Is it not to deal thy bread to the hungry, and that thou bring the poor that are cast out, when thou seest the naked, that thou cover him; and that thou hide not thyself from thine own flesh. Then shall thy light break forth as the morning, and thine health shall spring forth speedily: and thy righteousness shall go before thee; the glory of the Lord shall be thy reward."(Isaiah 58:6-8)

So what's on your breakfast plate for today? Is it scrambled eggs, a slice of toast, and a glass of orange juice? Or is it prayer, fasting and the word of God?

Jesus said that man shall not live by bread alone, but by every word of God(Luke 4:4) Let this day be the day when you rededicate your life to the almighty God. Sacrifice your body unto him in prayer and fasting, relinquish the things that are not important to your spiritual walk with God. Be aware of your actions and what you speak! Challenge yourself to think positively, cast down every vain imaginations that will exalt itself against the spirit of God, and let the Word be your daily bread. It is absolutely necessary that you read daily, it's like having a plant and without water and sunlight. The water and sunlight are necessary for the plant to grow. When you read the word and pray, you are like a plant that's growing in good soil, spreading its branches and bearing fruits. If you are depressed or frustrated, I declare that every spirit of depression and frustration is broken off your life in the name of Jesus. It is not by might nor by power but by the Spirit of the Almighty God. I want you to just take a moment and give him praise "Hallelujah" glory be to the Most High, the Everlasting Father and the King of kings, the Lord of lords.

PRAISE AND WORSHIP

Praise and worship must be a part of your daily routine. The Lord inhabits the praises of his people. God is present and glorified when His people lift His name in honor. God enjoys our praise, our praise and true worship cause God to turn his face towards us. He open doors that the enemy shuts when he receives our praise, and he close doors when the enemy opens them. God draws nearer to us and bless us when we praise Him. Praise is a potent tool that restores us even when we are broken. The divine potency of praise can change us for the better by refocusing our affections, realigning our priorities, and cause us to be receptive to God's Holy Spirit. When the praises go up then the blessing come down! In Psalm 149:1 and 3, David says "praise ye the Lord sing unto Lord a new song, and his praise in the congregation of saints. Verse 3 says, Let them praise his name in the dance: let them sing praise unto him with the timbrel and harp.

Worship is an intimacy with you and your God. Worship mean to lay one's self before God in prostration or make obeisance, whether in order to express respect or to make supplication to him. It takes you in the holy of holies where you can find yourself basking in true love and adoration for him. Worship is just what happens between you and God. Children of God, just worship him in **spirit and in truth** because God is a Spirit and only spirit can worship spirit. We were created to worship God. As we worship him there are areas in our lives that he will reveal to us. Some of these areas need to be changed or corrected. The Lord reveals himself through our worship both individually or corporately. True worship changes the atmosphere wherever you are. God's presence in our worship brings conviction, healing, deliverance and set the captives free. It gives you access to his person and his glory. It sets the atmosphere for miracles, signs and wonders. When Paul and Silas were thrown in prison, they began to pray and sang praises unto God; and suddenly there was a great earthquake, and the foundation of the prison were shaken and immediately all the prison doors were opened and chains were loosed.

Your praise will cause your 'jail break'. You can be delivered from whatever situation that is holding you hostage or bound. God is about to break the prison bars and set you free. Wherever you are right now, just take a moment and praise him for your deliverance and your breakthrough. True praise and worship comes from within. I want you find a secret place right now; if you need to change your location/position, do so now! Find your secret place of worship whether it is in your car on your way to work, bathroom, at lunch time on the job etc., I want you to focus on God. Think about what you need from God or what you want him to deliver you from. Imagine that you are in the presence of God right now. Begin to construct a mental picture of God stretching his arm towards you. Do you see him? Now, take a moment and just talk to him; it's like two people having a conversation. Begin to worship the Lord with praise that will cause him to release what he has in his hands for you. Thank him for what he is about to do for you. The Lord is listening to you right now, He wants to speak to you, but you have to be attentive to hear his voice. Stay focus for a moment and you will hear that *still small voice*. Conversations cannot be one sided. You cannot be the one who is always talking. Listen" listen!"

Having a personal relationship with him is the greatest honor that anyone can receive in life. Get to know the One you are serving at a personal level. He is waiting to embrace you, let him be the lover of your soul. There is none like him, no one can touch your heart like he can do. Let us fall in love with him all over again, let's renew our vows with our Creator and Master of our life.

When you're in a covenant relationship with God, it a commitment. Are you committed to him? God is a Covenant keeper! All you have to do is to keep his statutes and honor him. He said, "come unto me all who are heavy laden and I will give you rest." Put your head on his shoulders, Elohim love for you surpasses all human understanding, and for that reason, he sent is son to die for our sin. His unfailing love towards us has never failed. He is our shelter in the time of storm, he is able to keep that which we have committed unto him against that day. He is more than enough, therefore nothing can separate us from the love of Jesus Christ. He is omnipresent, always with you! He said he will never leave you or forsake you even until the end of the earth. Tt is God's desire that we prosper and be in good health. Do not be afraid of the terror by night: nor for the arrow that flieth by day; nor for the pestilence that walketh in darkness; nor for the destruction that wasteth at noonday. A thousand shall fall at thy side and ten thousand at thy right hand; but it shall not come nigh thee." Hallelujah" hallelujah" blessed be the name of the Lord. God has given you the victory, the weapon is formed but it cannot prosper! Luke 10:19 says," behold, I give unto you power to tread on serpents and scorpions, and over all the power of the enemy; and nothing shall by any means hurt you. I pray in the name of Jesus that any doors that the enemy has access to in your life, I command it shut and be sealed with the blood of Jesus.

Sin will cause doors to be opened to the enemy. Let your daily prayer includes repentance, David says it best in Psalms 51:1-3," have mercy upon me o Lord according to thy loving-kindness: according unto the multitude of thy tender mercies blot out my transgressions. Wash me thoroughly from mine iniquity, and cleanse me from my sin. For I acknowledge my transgressions: and my sin is ever before me." Acknowledging your sin and ask for forgiveness is true repentance.

Paul says, in 2 Corinthians 7: 1 says *"Having therefore these promises, dearly beloved, let us cleanse ourselves from all filthiness of the flesh and spirit, perfecting holiness in the fear of God".* Children of God let us strive for perfection. Paul also says in Hebrews 4: 15-16, *"For we have not an high priest which cannot be touched with the feeling of our infirmities; but was in all points tempted like as we are, yet without sin. Let us therefore come boldly unto the throne of grace that we may obtain mercy, and find grace to help in time of need.'*

I pray in the name of Jesus Christ that you will allow the spirit of God to destroy the yokes that are pulling you down, and lift the burdens that you are carrying. May he put your heart and mind at rest! "Hallelujah!" As you continue to walk in his anointing and grace you will be elevated in your season in the name of Jesus. Stop for a moment and just thank him for all that he has done for you! God has been good to us even when we don't deserve it, he is the Way Maker. Thank him for HIs grace and mercy that has brought you this far because this same grace is going to take you into your destiny in Jesus name. Trust in the Lord, your creator with all thine heart and lean not to thine own understanding but in all thy ways, acknowledge him and he shall direct thy path. Seek God daily for direction, in all thy ways acknowledge him and seek his guidance. A child depends on his parent for guidance and protection each day. Likewise, we must depend on our Heavenly father to guide and protect us as we travel along this pathway.

BEING CHOSEN BY GOD AND THE PROCESS INTO MATURITY

It is easy for us to stand and say, I am a chosen vessel of God but there's a process that we have to go through. There is a wilderness experience where you feel all alone, rejected, empty, sad, persecuted, and forsaken. Sometimes you might be led to wonder why God chose to use you as a vessel when you were minding your own business, without even thinking about him. I remembered when I just got saved. I lifted my hands to heaven and said," use me Lord! Send me! I will go where ever you send me! I'm yours Lord, use me (because I've found true love). At that time, I did not knowing that I was just sealing what was already been predestined for my life. Sometimes, we ask and pray for things that we have no idea about what we really asked for. If we ask with sincerity in faith, God will truly reward you. As I grew

27

in faith, I realize that the hand of God is upon me. The truth is that God has already chosen me even before I was conceived in my mother's womb.

When you are born again, you have to learn how to crawl as babies. You are fed with milk which is the word, which is nourishment to your strength and growth. As you begin to grow, you will learn to stand on your own. Your milk will gradually turn into meat as you grow and develop into maturity. However, you will still need the guidance of your parents (**stay with me in the spirit**). You take a step but you are still not strong enough, so you fall back to the ground. But, because of your determination to walk, you will get up and try the process again. Since you really want to walk, you place your right foot forward but you are still a little shaky. You are not able to balance yourself because there are obstacles that you are still struggling with, and nervousness is taking control, but you keep trying! As you practice to walk and exercise your faith, you will realize that you are gaining strength each day. You are still fed with milk but a little piece of meat is added in between. You're not able to chew that well, but your still walking! Daily, you are been guided by leadership and now you are in toddler stage. The journey is long, but you are moving day by day. At times you might throw a little tantrum but you'll get through it with the help of God. (**Stay with me in the Spirit**).

God will strategically place people in your life for different seasons and for his purpose. When that season is finished, you have to discern and quit crying over spilled milk because it's the end of that season. As you grow, God will use situations to remove some people from your life in some cases, but not all. *Why is this so?* Because he knows that you would not have loose yourself from that relationship, so he has to use things or people to remove them out of your life. Isn't it amazing how we can hold on to people and things that God is trying to pull away from us? Holding on to them will only hinder your blessings and prevent you from moving forward in God. A perfect example is Abraham and Lot. God will take something from you to give you something better, and he can do whatever he wants to do with us because he is our Father, and there is nothing you can do about it! So get with his program, He is God all by himself." The Book of Genesis 1: 1 starts, "In the beginning, God...... hallelujah". On this journey, you also have to be self-disciplined. Know who you are and know your boundaries. There are lines that you just cannot cross and there are set standards in your journey, but you are equipped to empower today to bring a better tomorrow. There are different changes and seasons in your life, summer, fall, winter and spring. Look at the trees as they go through different seasons and changes! In the summer, the trees are full of leaves green and fresh, some bearing fruits and flowers. When that season is up there is fall, when the leaves start to shed its leaves and appeared to be dried up. Then comes winter where it's cold, frigid and gloomy, after which spring rolls in where everything starts to grow back.

Psalms 1:3 David says, *"and he shall be like a tree planted by the rivers of water, that bringeth fruits in his season; his leaves also shall not wither; and whatsoever he doeth shall prosper"*.

Be patient, do not be dismayed, you are been pruned, he is setting you up for greatness. Know what season you are in, so you can be better prepared spiritually, mentally and physically. Go through your seasons with the assurance that it will change. Stay in prayer and fasting, you will be empowered from on high! Trust in the Lord and he will carry you through, make no provision for yourself he already knows what you need. The Bible says in Matthew 6: 8 says, "for your Father knoweth what things ye have need of, before ye ask him and he is able to deliver you out of any situation".

He is the Author and the Finisher of your faith. If you stick by him, he will stick by you because he is a faithful God. Every drop of blood that was shed was for you, signifies how much he loves you.

Father in the name of Jesus Christ I command everything that you have ordained and predestine for your children's life to come in alignment with your words according to Isaiah 55:10-11. For as the rain cometh down, and the snow from heaven, and returneth not thither, but watereth the earth and maketh it bring forth and bud, that it may give seed to the sower, and bread to the eater. So shall my word be that goeth forth out of my mouth: it shall not return unto me void, but it shall accomplish that which I please, and it shall prosper in the thing whereto I sent it. If they have taken any detour, they will allow you to be their navigational system to take them back on the right path amen.

Children of God, let go the steering wheel and give it to Jesus. Let him direct you because that's the only way you will fulfill your destiny. There is no short cut on this journey. There is a song that says, *"It a hard road to travel and a mighty long way to go"*. This journey is not easy! This road is a narrow, rocky one, but Jesus is our Way-maker.

There are proper protocols that has to be followed in order to reach where God wants you to be at a certain time in your life. You will get to the right path if you stay connected to the spirit of God (the vine, the source). God has never failed me yet and he is no respecter of person. What he did for me he can do it for you! He is your shepherd, David said in Psalm 23:1-3, *the Lord is my shepherd; I shall not want. He maketh me to lie down in green pastures: he leadeth me beside the still waters. He restoreth my soul: he leadeth me in the path of righteousness for his name's sake.* The Lord will lead us in green pastures green pastures so that we can sit by still waters. His name is above every other name. Acts 4:12 stated that, "Neither is there salvation in any: for there is none other name under heaven given among man, whereby we must be saved." At the name of Jesus, every knee shall bow and ever tongue shall confess that Jesus Christ is Lord.

There is power in is name and you can call him any time you need him. When you call him, he will come to your rescue. He is a friend that sticks closer than a brother. Friendship with Jesus is divine and priceless. There is no amount of money in this world that can be of any value than your friendship with your Heavenly Father. Jesus Christ cannot be compared to any form of worldliness or earthly possession. He is from everlasting to everlasting; the Prince of Peace Emmanuel, El-Shaddai, Elohim, Omniscient, Omnipresent, Omnipotent, Alpha and Omega. You can count on him, he will carry you through because he is no respecter of persons.

God is a just God. There is no favoritism in him; He is not like man and only you can prevent him from meeting your need is if you doubt his power or underestimate what he can do. Here now, children of God, listen and be obedient to his instructions because he knows what is best for you. Do not try to instruct God, especially when you pray. Ask him to have his will and his way in your life! He said whatsoever you ask in my name you can have it, but sometimes we ask for the wrong things. Let go and let God take over and direct your path. He will strengthen you when you don't feel like you can go on. We are children of light but sometimes the flesh wants to take charge of our lives. As children of God, let us feed our spirit with the Word of God and spend time in prayer and fasting. Yes, it's a daily fight between the spirit and the flesh, but it depends on which one you feed the most. ***Are you giving attention to the flesh or the Spirit?***

CHANGING YOUR MINDSET

The Apostle Paul exhorts us in Philippians 4:8 by saying," finally, brethren, whatsoever thing are true, whatsoever things are honest, whatsoever things are just, whatsoever things are pure, whatsoever things are lovely, whatsoever things are of good report; if there be any virtue, and if there be any praise, think on these things".

The mind is a central source of the body; it is where your thoughts, emotions and actions are activated. Your action is reflection of your thoughts, SO A MAN THINKETH, SO IS HE. Your thought process can be a hindrance to your blessing and your destiny. The words of the late and great legendary, Robert Nester Marley (aka Bob Marley) a song writer, reggae music composer and producer says, **"emancipate yourself from mental slavery none but our self can free our mind"** (words from Redemption Song). You have the will power with the grace of God to free your own mind!

The infamous Willie Lynch (a British slave owner in the West Indies) wrote a letter entitled, '*The making of a slave*'. Lynch's personal occupation was a horse trainer. A part of Lynch's method of controlling slaves was to program their minds to savvier oppression. He used fear, distrust and envy for controlling purpose. A horse at an early age of its life is bridled and trained to learn and to adapt to its environment. When we were sinners, we train ourselves to adapt to the things of the world. Our life style mirrors the things of the environment in which we interact. Likewise, when we have fully dedicated our lives to Christ, we become a part of his kingdom, we have to adapt to the mandates and precepts that are found in the Bible.

In Roman 12:1-2, the Apostle Paul wrote, "I beseech you therefore brethren, by the mercies of God, that ye present your bodies a living sacrifice, holy, acceptable unto God, which is your reasonable service; and be not conformed to this world: but be ye transform by the renewing of your mind, that ye may prove what is that perfect, will of God". The Bible also encourages us in Ephesians 4:23, that you must be renewed in the spirit of your mind.

1 Peter 1:13 says" wherefore gird up the loins of your mind, be sober, and hope to the end for the grace that is to be brought unto you at the revelation of Jesus Christ". The enemy wants to mess with your mind and if he gets your mind, then he can control you. You mind is the enemy's main target but he is afraid of your faith.

2 Corinthians 10:4-5 states that, *the weapon of our warfare are not carnal, but mighty through God for the pulling down of strong holds Casting down imagination and every high thing that exalted itself against the knowledge of God, and bringing into captivity every thought to the obedience of Christ.*

I pray in the name of Jesus Christ that there will be a shift in your mindset that will catapult you forward in God. I command by the authority of Jesus Christ, that from now on, your thinking process will be changed. I call your mind, soul, and body to be in alignment with Christ Jesus. Aspire to renew your mind because it's not by might nor by power but by the Spirit of the Lord. Rise and command a shift! Lay hands on yourself and speak into your mind. Life and death is in the power of the tongue hallelujah" Right now, just take a moment and give him thanks, praise be to the Most High the Almighty God who reigns forever more. You are victorious, you can do all things through Christ that strengthen you. You are a winner! Say; "I am a winner, I am victorious!" Say it like you meant it in Jesus name, amen.

TAKING AUTHORITY OVER THE ENEMY

It is time for us to take authority over the enemy. You have allowed the enemy to beat you down too long! The enemy has been holding you in bondage for a long time. Let us be reminded that he is the prince of the air who has no authority on earth. Therefore, we must not allow him to take control over our lives. *For the weapons of warfare are not carnal but mighty through God for the pulling down of strong hold, we wrestle not against flesh and blood but against principality and power against the rulers of darkness against spiritual wickedness in high places.* Know who is the real enemy. Satan is the real culprit who organizes the plots and plans to destroy us. We have to be able to discern his tactics so that we can put him to shame when he tries to crawl his way into our path. The enemy will always try to distract you, he never gives up! He will use the people around you to destroy you but, they are not the real enemy. They are just the vessel that have made themselves available to be used by him (the devil). I encourage you to stay in prayer and fasting, these are powerful weapons against the enemy. The enemy cannot touch you unless God gives him permission to do so. Look at Job for example, Satan could not touch him until God gave him permission. God took the edge of protection from around Job so that his faith could be tested. Do not be afraid of the enemy God has not given you the spirit of fear but of love and a sound mind! TAKE AUTHORITY OVER THE ENEMY, USE YOUR WEAPON!!

David mentioned in Psalms 91: 1 that, he who dwells in the secret place of the most high shall abide under the shadow of the Almighty. When we stay in the secret place of God, he will protect us and his angels will encamp around us. Psalms 91 also says, A thousand shall fall at thy side, and ten thousand at thy right hand; but it shall not come nigh thee. O what a sweet assurance to understand that our life is in God's mighty hand!

He has given his angel charge over you there are angels that assign to you stay connected to the source which is Jesus Christ. He is your shield and butler, you can rise above ever circumstances that has come up against you in the name of Jesus Christ. Use his name! Victory belongs to you, Jesus went to the cross for you and his blood covers you. He will never leave you or forsake you, because you are a child of the King and he will take care of you. His word will not return to him void but it will accomplish what he has spoken over your life. Do not be dismayed, *the weapon can form but it will not prosper* because you are a child of the King of kings.

.... *and every tongue that shall rise against thee in judgment thou shalt condemn. This is the heritage of the servants of the Lord and their righteousness is of me, saith the Lord* (Isaiah 54:17). The Only True and Living God is able to keep you from falling and present you faultless with exceeding joy. You are victorious through Christ Jesus! Surrender your all and submit your will to him because the enemy is defeated. Run your course and keep the faith, and take your eyes off what the enemy is doing. Laugh at the storm because the hotter the battle, the sweeter the victory.

BEING ANOINTED BY GOD AND WALKING IN THE ANOINTING

Let us first acknowledge the one who has anointed us. The only true and living God, Jehovah the Great I am! The same God that raise Lazarus from the dead! The Messiah-*the*

Anointed One, has anointed you for a purpose. You have to seek him to know what that purpose is. You are anointed to do a particular task, the spirit of God will lead you; it's not by might nor by power but by his spirit. The anointing is the enabler who helps you to do the things that you would seems humanly impossible to do. The anointing will enable you to comprehend the things that would be incomprehensible or intellectually-challenging to man. It takes faith to walk in the anointing that God has put upon your life, as a matter of fact, when you said 'YES' to GOD, faith-walk begins. We walk by faith and not by sight. You are been led by God. You can't see him but you can feel him. Do not look on your situations around you, they are just temporary, they are only for a moment. The battle is not yours, it's the Lord's. He will not put more on you than you can manage. In all your ways acknowledge him and he shall direct your path. He will lead you into still waters. The storm may be rough right now; Peter said, if it is you Lord bid me to come." Jesus said, "**come, step into the deep.**" When you walk with your Savior, you can never miss your season, and he will not fail you if you let him lead you beside still waters.

There are people waiting for you! There may be someone that's about to commit suicide or going through some hard times who just need an encouraging word from you. The Lord can lead you to that person right on time to save them from the spirit of suicide. A word from God will propel you into your destiny, press on my brothers and sister in Christ to the mark of the prize of the higher calling. Paul said in Philippians 3:10-14, "that I may know him, and the power of his resurrection, and the fellowship of his sufferings, being made conformable unto his death. If by any means I might attain unto the resurrection of the dead. Not as though I had already perfect: but I follow after, if that I may apprehend that for which also I am apprehended of Christ Jesus. Brethren, I count not myself to have apprehend: but this one thing I do, forgetting those things which are behind, and reaching forth unto those things which are before, I press toward the mark for the prize of the high calling of God in Christ Jesus".

Psalm 24:7 says" lift up your heads o ye gates; and be ye lift up, ye everlasting doors; and the King of glory shall come in. Who is this King of glory, the Lord strong and mighty, the Lord mighty in battle."

You have a father who already fought and won your battles for you. Yes, you've already won! He took up on himself, all our burdens at the cross. Keep on walking by faith and not by sight. He will carry you through, you will come up against opposition but know that God is with you even unto the end. David says in Psalms 116:8), "for thou hast delivered my soul from death, mine eyes from tears and my feet from falling. In verse 12, he said what shall I render unto the Lord for all his benefits towards me, I will take the cup of salvation, and call upon the name of the Lord".

Your destiny can be affected by the decisions you make along the way, but it cannot be altered by anyone or anything. It is sealed by God your creator. Only you can stop what he was predestined for your life by not walking in obedience. Let the will of the Lord be done in your life! Be obedient to him. For obedience is better than sacrifice! Listen for his instruction along the way and take heed to his word. Let him be your guide, his amazing grace will keep you. In all thy ways acknowledge him and he shall direct your path. His word is a lamp unto your feet and a light unto your path. You belong to him and he has set you free, you are no longer bound, for his love will carry you all the way. AMEN.

John 3:16 says *"For God so loved the world, that he gave his only begotten son, that whosoever believeth in him should not perish, but have everlasting life"*

BEING PERSECUTED FOR RIGHTEOUSNESS SAKE

Being lied on, talked about, being mistreated and abused, being misused, being looked down on, the ridicule, the rejection: It took me a while to understand that persecution was a part of the process, it is a part of the journey. Being persecuted for righteousness sake prepares me to be ready for ministry! It prepared ME for what was going to come- *the anointing that is on my life.* 2 Timothy 3:12 and all that will live Godly in Christ Jesus shall suffer persecution. In 2 Corinthians 12:9 -10, Paul sought the Lord thrice about the thorn in his flesh. In other words, Paul sought after God for deliverance. ***And the Lord said my grace is sufficient for thee: for my strength is made perfect in weakness.*** Because of God's grace Paul said, *"most gladly therefore will I rather glory in my infirmities, that the power of Christ may rest upon me. Therefore I take pleasure in infirmities, in reproach, in necessities, in persecution, in distresses for Christ's sakes: for when I am weak, then I am strong".*

If you are going through persecution, being lied on, laughed at, misused, abused, look down on, don't be despair because everything work together for good for them that love the Lord, to them who are called according to his purpose.

In Romans 8:35, the Apostle Paul asked, "Shall tribulation, or distress, or persecution, or famine, or nakedness, or peril, or sword?" Yes sometimes the enemy will use people to get to you. On the flip side, God may be working something out for you or building you up to do what he has called you to do. The greater the anointing, the greater the warfare and the persecution. You will go through persecution as long as you are living for God.

1 Peter 5:6 says humble yourselves therefore under the mighty hand of God, that he may exalt you in due time. I know it hurts when persecution comes because we are human and the flesh will fail you. Don't be distracted by what people is doing to you. Just keep your eyes on God because at the end of this life, you have to give an account for your own life, stay in prayer and fasting!

In Jude 1:20, the Bible says" *But ye, beloved, building up yourselves on your most holy faith, prayer in the Holy Ghost*". Keep your heart pure before God our Lord and Savior Jesus Christ and he will fight your battles because the battle is not yours it is the Lord's.

Father I pray that whatsoever your children is going through, they will surrender it to you and let you be their battle axe in this season in the name of Jesus; because the battle is yours. Lord I pray that they will not lean on their own understanding. Your word says the weapon of our warfare are not carnal but mighty through God for the pulling down of stronghold. Have your way Jehovah -Nissi, Our Banner. You are the same God yesterday, today, and forever more. The same God that delivers the children of Israel out of bondage and lead them into the promise land, is the same God of Daniel, Abraham, and Moses. Deliver your people O God, because you are the God that never change. Jesus have your way amen.

THE CRAFTINESS OF MANKIND IN THE CHURCHES TODAY

Some churches today have become religious entities to showcase talents and gifts rather than having a people who hunger and thirst after God. Some brethren including leaders who function in various prestigious and high profiled assignments, as well as other members have diverted from the main focus of the church. There seems to be a shift from yearning to be righteous and holy to yearning to become crafty and worldly. The love of money, and the wearing of expensive name brands, selling of the gospel, charging money for prophecies, miracles and deliverance are now displaying price tags that cost large fortunes. The church is no longer considered a hospital where the lost and needy would go for help or relief. Churches have now become a business place, it has become a den of thieves, a market place.

The Bible sates in John 2:13-16 that 'the Jews Passover was at hand, and Jesus went up to Jerusalem, and found in the temple those that sold oxen and sheep and doves, and the changers of money sittings: and when he had made a scourge of small cords, he drove them all out of the temple, and the sheep, and oxen; and poured out the chargers' money, and overthrew the tables; and said unto them that sold doves, Take these things hence; make not my Father's house an house of merchandise'.

There are some 'self-appointed' leaders who see the church as an opportunity to make money in the name of Jesus. Woe onto them that are using the Word of God to their advantage to rob God's people! It is imperative that you break up your fallow ground. 2 Corinthians 4:2 renounced the hidden things of dishonesty, not walking in craftiness, commending ourselves to every man's conscience in the sight of God.

In Ephesians 4:14, Paul states that we as the body of Christ need to unite so that 'we henceforth be no more children, tossed to and fro and carried about with every wind of doctrine, by the sleight of man and cunning craftiness whereby they lie in wait to deceive'.

In Matthew 24, Jesus sat upon the Mount of Olives and told his disciples when they asked him what shall be the signs of thy coming, and of the end of the world, Jesus told them to take heed that no man deceive them. He said," for many shall come in my name saying I am Christ; and shall deceive many". He went on to say, *"if any man shall say unto you here is Christ believe it not for there shall arise false Christ's, and false prophets and you shall see sign and wonder insomuch that, if it were possible they shall deceive the very elect"*. Now, I am saying to you, "be alert my brothers and sisters in Christ, be watchful try the spirit by the spirit to see if it is of God. Do not be deceived, do not go by what you feel *(this is of the flesh)* but rather use the Spirit to discern.

There are some men and women of God who have whole heartedly given their lives to the Lord, and have fully surrendered and avail themselves so that God can use them. They have presented their bodies as a living sacrifice and have decided they will not sell the gospel or put a price on the anointing that God has given to them. There is no amount of money in this world that can buy the anointing, it is not to be sold! In the book of Acts Chapter 3:1-6 it declares that," *Now Peter and John went up together into the temple at the hour of prayer, being the ninth hour. And a certain man lame from his mother's womb was carried, whom they laid daily at the gate at the temple which is call Beautiful to ask alms of them that enter into the temple; who seeing Peter and John about to go in the temple asked an alms. And Peter, fastening his eyes upon him with John, said Look on us. And he gave heed unto them, expecting to receive something of them. Then Peter said, Silver and gold have I none; but such as I have give I thee: In the name of Jesus Christ of Nazareth rise up and walk. And he told him by the right hand, and lifted him up: and immediately his feet and ankle bones received strength. And he leaping up stood, and walked, and entered with them into the temple walking, and leaping, and praising God".*

Freely you receive, freely you give back! The anointing is not for you, it is for the people whether saved and unsaved. Yes, there are some men and women of God who are sold out and will not compromise the word of God. The Bible says, 'Thou hast a few names even in Sardis which have not defiled their garments; and they shall walk with me in white: for they are worthy" (Revelation 3:4). These are the ones that will trust God to meet the needs of the church as well as their personal needs without indulging in any form of craftiness. Money is needed to effectively run the church, and all eyes are upon church leaders to spearhead this mission. No church should be closed because of lack of finances, therefore tithes and offerings must be paid to fulfill this need. Money is needed for the church to function, the doors of the church must be kept opened, and the burdens must not be solely left on the pastors. Electricity bills must be paid, rent/mortgage has to be paid, and your pastor should not lack anything. In other words, all expenses must be addressed and paid. It is important to pay your tithes and offering. Yes! You need to **give back to God what he has given you.** God will supply not some but, **ALL** your needs according to his riches in glory.

Malachi 3:7-12 said return *unto me and I will return unto you, saith the lord of hosts. But ye said, wherein shall we return? Will a man rob God? Yet ye have robbed me. But ye say, wherein have we robbed thee? In tithes and offerings. Ye are cursed with a curse: for ye have robbed me, even this whole nation. Bring ye all the tithes into the storehouse, that there may be meat in mine house, and prove me now herewith, said the Lord of hosts, if I will not open you the windows of heaven, and pour you out a blessing, that there shall not be room enough to receive it. And I will rebuke the devourer for your sakes, and he shall not destroy the fruits of your ground; neither shall vine cast her fruit before the time in the field, saith the Lord of hosts. And all nations shall call you blessed: for ye shall be a delightsome land, said the Lord of hosts.*

Saints of God, pray for your leaders. I beseech you saints of God to pray for them and their families. They need your prayers, the enemy goes after the head first. If the enemy hits the shepherd, the sheep will scatter that's why they need your prayer. Moses had Aaron and Hur (a King of the Midianites) held on to God's hands up in battle against the Amalekite. Keep on praying for your leaders, keep on holding their hands up high, it is not by might nor by power but by the spirit of God. When you take care of God's business than he will take care of yours, Amen.

THE ROAD TO RECOVER THAT WHICH WAS LOST

It is so important to seek guidance daily from the Lord Jesus Christ. Beloved it is imperative to our Christian walk with God, children need daily guidance from their parents, and you also need daily guidance from your Heavenly Father. Many of you have lost many things along your journey. Some of you have missed your season simply because you weren't paying attention to what God is saying to you. Sin, being disobedient, reluctant to do the will of the Lord, or just hanging with the wrong crowd can cause you to miss your season. Our merciful God will redeem the times as long as we repent and turn from our wicked ways. Submit your will to his will and he will allow you everything you have lost, he will allow you to recover all.

Joel 2:25 says, "And I will restore to you the years that the locust eaten, the cankerworm, and the caterpillar, and the palmerworm, my great army which I sent among you."

God promises not only to restore what was lost, but to restore it abundantly. ... You will have plenty to eat, until you are full, and you will praise the name of the Lord your God, who has worked wonders for you; never again will my people be ashamed. This is a sweet promise for anyone who has suffered the consequences of their sin and fears that they cannot recover what was lost. God is a kind and merciful Father to us who will not discipline us more than is necessary and longs to restore us in our relationship to him, and in the blessings we enjoyed by his hand.

The Lord is not slack concerning his promise, as some men count slackness; but is longsuffering to us-ward, not willing that any should perish, but that all should come to repentance.(**2 Peter 9**)

In 2 Chronicle 7:13-14 the Bible says, "If I shut up heaven that there be no rain, or if I command the locust to devour the land, or if I send pestilence among my people; If my people, which are call by my name, shall humble themselves, and pray, and seek my face, and turn from their wicked ways; then will I hear from heaven, and will forgive their sin, and will heal their land".

God purpose and plan for you does not change but man can change their minds about you. God is not a man that he should lie if he said **IT**, it must come to pass. God's love for us is unconditional and authentic. When you repent and turn your heart back to him he is obligated to do what he said he will do.

In 1 Peter 5:10 the Bible says," But the God of all grace, who hath called us unto his eternal glory by Christ Jesus, after that ye have suffered a while, make you perfect, stablish, strengthen, settle you".

SPIRITUAL PYRAMID THE FIVE LEVEL ACCESS IN THE REALM OF THE SPIRIT -

Father& Son

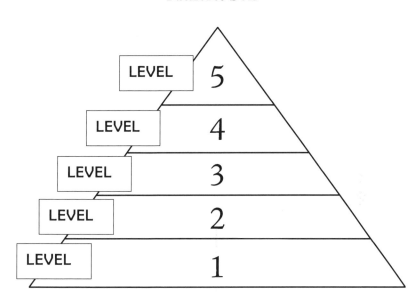

LEVEL 1

REVELATION KNOWLEDGE FROM GOD

Special revelation is the knowledge of God and spiritual matters which can be discovered through supernatural means, such as scripture or miracles by individuals. Direct revelation refers to communication from God to someone in particular.

The revelation knowledge from God cannot be attained through philosophical, or the merely human powers of reason and inquiry, but through God's revelation in Scriptures. It is reading of the Word and your act of faith in God when you meditate on his word. This revelation will help you to realize that there is a higher power, a higher entity, a higher supernatural being! The principle of God's word is been shown to you through the Holy Spirit. Your spiritual eyes is been enlightened (opened) to understand and to receive what you could not have known on your own because God reveal it to you through reading the word. The spirit of God gives the revelation when you meditate on his Word.

Hebrews 4:12 says; "for the word of God is quick, and powerful, and sharper than any two-edged sword, piercing even to the dividing asunder of soul and spirit, and of the joints and marrow, and is a discerner of the thoughts and intents of the heart." So the word starts to guide you, mold you, it shifts you into position, it starts to capture your mind and become rooted in your heart.

The word of God guides you; the word of God becomes your daily GPS. The scripture says **it's a lamp unto my feet and a light unto my path.** The word of God will help you to understand that places you used to go, you cannot go there anymore. When you study the word of God, you will not have the desire to do the things that you used to do. Even if you find yourself in the wrong places or doing the wrong things, the Holy Spirit will convict you until you get uncomfortable. During conviction, it is you who will make the decision to either submit or not submit to the spirit of God. There is no conviction when you have fully surrendered your life to the devil. *"And the LORD said, My spirit shall not always strive with man........"(Genesis 6:3)*

Yet, God who is so merciful may send someone with a word for you! This word may come through the voice of pastor preaching the word of God, a prophet, someone close to you, someone who doesn't even know you, or even a little child for that matter. It is not the will of the Lord for anyone to perish but all should come to repentance. Jesus says, "I came not to call the righteous, but sinners to repentance" (Luke 5:32)

The word molds you: In the book Romans 12:1, Paul the Apostle states, "I beseech you therefore brethren, by the mercies of God that you present your bodies a living sacrifice, holy, acceptable unto God, which is your reasonable service." In 11 Chronicles 6: 13 states that when Solomon finished building the temple, he made an altar and present himself unto God as a sacrifice. When you give your life to the Lord, he takes control of it! Your body becomes the temple of the Holy Spirit, a dwelling place for the Holy Spirit to reside. The truth is that the Lord reveals to redeem. The sinful nature of man will allow him (man) to lay at the altar if he is truly convicted by the Holy Spirit through the word of God. Studying and meditating on the word will cause us to change our lifestyle, attitude, behavior, mindset, speech, and appetite to yearn after the things of God. These changes will allow you to take on the very nature of God; your appearance changes, your countenance changes, your attitude toward people changes! Submission is the key to transformation, remember you can only hinder yourself.

THE WORD OF GOD SHIFTS YOU INTO POSITION FOR HIS PURPOSE:

The more you read or hear the word of God and act upon it, the more it will work on your mind, thoughts and your action. So once there is a shift in your mind, you must shift position! You are reposition into his will for your life because the word challenges you to grow. John 1:1 says," In the beginning was the word and the word was with God, and the word was God". So God will shift you into position for his purpose, shift is designed for you to grow, shift challenges you to be mature, shift requires rethinking, redefining, shifts require you to let go off something in order to embrace something else, it ushers you into something new.

Matthew 9: 16-17 KJV says, "No man putteth a piece of new cloth unto an old garment, for that which is put in to fill it up taketh from the garment, and rent is made worst. Neither do men put new wine into old bottles: else the bottles break, and the wine runneth out, and the bottles perish: but they put new wine into new bottles, and both are preserved". The NIV version translates this same Matthew 9:16-17 as, "No one sews a patch of unshrunk cloth on an old garment, for the patch will pull away from the garment, making the tear worse. Neither do man pour new wine into old wineskins will be ruined. No, they pour new wine into new wineskins, and both are preserved."

So God will take you from places, people and things to give you something better, to shift you into his will and position you for purpose. We don't understand what God is doing when we are going through rough and trying times, and so you may try to hold on to people, place and things, you try to hold on to what you think you know. But God wants you to let go so he can bring you to a place where you can learn something new. Let go and let God have his way in your life! He said eyes have not seen the thing he has prepared for you. Isaiah 55:8 -11 says, "For my thoughts are not your thoughts, neither are your ways my ways, saith the Lord. For as the heavens are higher than the earth, so are my ways and my thoughts than your thoughts. For as the rain cometh down, and the snow from heaven, and returneth not thither, but watereth the earth, and maketh it bring forth and bud, that it may give seed to the sower, and bread to the eater: so shall my word be that goeth forth out of my mouth: it shall not return unto me void, but it shall accomplish that which I please, and it shall prosper in the thing whereto I sent it."

Jeremiah 29: 11 "For I know the thoughts that I think towards you, saith the lord, thoughts of peace, and not of evil, to give you an expected end.

LEVEL 2

REVEALING ACT OF GOD

In Exodus chapter 3, God revealed himself to Moses in the burning bush, Jesus fed five thousand with five loaves of bread and three fishes, Moses parted the Red Sea for the children of Israel. God used many different ways to reveal himself to his people, God will reveal himself to you through dreams, vision, the written word through time and space. He stepped out of eternity into time and manifest himself through the flesh Jesus Christ for our sin, he revealed himself through Jesus Christ so shall it be even now. God will reveal himself to you! He said, I am going, but I will sent the Comforter, the Holy Spirit. You are the righteousness of God.

In Genesis 1:26 -27 God said, let us make man in our image, after our likeness: and let them have dominion over the fish of the sea, and over the fowl of the air, and over the cattle, and over all the earth, and over every creeping thing that creepeth upon the earth. God created man in his own image, in the image of God created he; male and female created he them.

So God will reveal himself through you, he said you will lay hands on the sick and they will recover because he is Jehovah Rapha our healer and his healing power is in you. So the revealing act of God comes through you, he said he has given you power to trample upon serpents and scorpions and they shall not harm you. Your act of faith will allow God to reveal himself in you. Ephesians 4: 6 says; One God and father of all, who is above all, and through all and in you all.

The Lord asked Moses in Exodus Chapter 4, "what is that in thine hand? And Moses said a rod, God used the very rod that Moses had to demonstrate his power and to reveal his deity to Moses (his divine character or nature). There are gifts that God has given you, the word of God says his gifts are without repentance. He will not take back what he has given you. You can be gifted but have no anointing. It is the anointing that makes the difference. It is the anointing that destroy the yoke, and he will use it to reveal his act. If you walk by his principles and be obedient to him he will use you to demonstrate his power so that the unbeliever could see and know that we serve a powerful and mighty God. He is still the same God yesterday, today and forever more because he changes not. He is the same God of Abraham, Isaac and Jacob. Man changes but God never change. He is an awesome God! The scripture said *come taste and see that the Lord is good.* He will show you a glimpse of where he is taking you, but there are things that you are going to encounter to get to the end result. God knows how much you can handle; sometimes he will show you little by little to encourage you when you get weary or send a word whether by a prophet, pastor, the written word or through situations. God is always speaking it's for you to pay attention, to see or to hear.

LEVEL 3

WARRING ANGELS

Warring angels or princes of heaven are to help the children of God in extreme, dangerous situations (2 Kings 6:18-19); such as the time Elisha stood on the side of a mountain with the Syrian army surrounding him. Warring angels wage war in actual combat engagement. They are activating angelic messengers whose assignment is to protect you and your loved ones; while they are supernatural, unseen beings that ensure they are with you especially in times of need. They are the celestial attendants of God, the divine messengers of God, heavenly beings, guardians, they are God's agents. God will give you access to enter into the realm of the spirit that when you pray, he hears and send out angels to enforce order. When the righteous cry, the Lord hears him and answers. Since GOD is the Giver of gifts, He is the one that places the anointing upon your life and each person's anointing is different.

Someone may want to ask, *"But what is the anointing?* "The Anointing is the indwelling presence of the Holy Spirit in the life of a believer. It enables the believer to understand, apply, and administer spiritual truth. Simply put, the presence of The Anointing enables believers to have a spiritual connection. The Holy Spirit indwells us and allows us to connect to the spiritual realm so that we can receive and understand spiritual data as it is transferred from heaven to earth. The spiritual receptivity that comes as a result of The Anointing allows us to maintain fellowship with God because of the presence of the Holy Spirit. The Anointing allows us to discern truth from error. It is a detector that allows us to know right from wrong.

We all carry different 'weight' in the realm of the spirit. What do I mean by your weight the realms of the spirit? In first chapter of the book of Job when satan was going to and fro on the earth, God said to him, "Have you considered my servant Job?" This means that Job carried a lot of weight. Does the enemy know your name? There are different types of angel with different assignments depending on the situation. When Peter was captured and put in prison, they gave him a death sentence; they join together at Mary's home and start to pray for his release. In response to their prayers, God send an angel to break him out of prison. It was the second time that God sent an angel to release Peter out of prison (see Acts 5: 18-25). When we pray, God responds. It could be instant or a waiting period or there are unseen forces sent out to stop or block God's response. But, your God, Jehovah Gibbor, has given you the authority he has given you a voice to bind, to loose, and to speak the Word!

Acts 12: 21-24 reads, "And upon a set day Herod, arrayed in royal apparel, sat upon his throne, and made an oration unto them. And the people gave a shout, saying, it is the voice of a God, and not of man. And immediately the Angel of the Lord smote him, because he gave not God the Glory: and he was eaten of worms, and gave up the ghost. But the word of God grew and multiplied."

LEVEL 4

HIGHER DEPTHS IN GOD

An elevation is when you have learned and mastered the act of faith in God. When you have accomplished spiritual intelligence (manifestation of a high mental capacity) in God, you have the power and the ability to do whatever he has given you to do. You can now do the things that once seem impossible to the natural eyes and to man. You are anointed for that purpose, your anointing will prepared you for your assignment. When you are anointed to carry out a specific assignment, God will equip you with the grace to do your task. It is not by might nor by power but by the Spirit of God! The Lord will entrust you with things after he has tested you and find you faithful. 1 Peter 5:6 and 10 says" *Humble yourselves under God's mighty hand, that he may lift you up in due time. But the God of all grace, who hath called us unto his eternal glory by Christ Jesus, after you have suffered a while, make you perfect, stablish, strengthen, settle you.*"

No matter what you are going through, meditate on these word knowing that everything is working out for the greater good. Though the vision tarries, wait because it is for an appointed time it must come to pass, embrace the testing and trials because all things work together for good to them that love the Lord and our savior Jesus Christ. 1 Peter 3:17-18 says, "***For it is better, if*** *the will of God be so, that ye suffer for well doing, than for evil doing. For Christ also hath once suffered for sins, the just for the unjust, that he might bring us to God, being put to death in the flesh, but quickened by the Spirit".*

Suffering is a must for believers. There is no way around it. Jesus came and suffered for our sins so shall we also go through much suffering for him. A famous Christian author, Watchman Nee, documented in one of his books that, *"there is no gold which has not passed through fire, no precious stone that has not gone through darkness, and no pearl that has not encountered suffering".*

The Apostle Paul states in 2 Corinthians 12:7-10, *"And lest I should be exalted above measure through the abundance of the revelations, there was given to me a throne in the flesh, the messenger of satan to buffet me, lest I should be exalted above measure. For this thing I besought the Lord thrice, that it might depart from me. And he said unto me, my grace is sufficient for thee: for my strength is made perfect in weakness. Most gladly therefore will I rather glory in my infirmities, that the power of Christ may rest upon me. Therefore I take pleasure in infirmities, in reproaches, in necessities, in persecutions, in distresses for Christ's sakes: for when I am weak, then am I strong".*

No matter who you are, or the number of titles that you have, there is something that God will use to keep you humble before him. As believers, we must suffer for Christ sake; (you might be saying, well you know I have been walking this walk for a long time, it's time for God to give me a break) but your sufferings, afflictions, trials, persecutions are part of your walk with the Lord and Savior Jesus Christ.

Jesus suffered the cross and despise the shame for you and me. So, continue to carry your daily cross, rejoice for the steps of a righteous man are ordered by the Lord. As long as you're in the land of the living you will suffer, remember that this present suffering or affliction is only for a moment.

In 2 Corinthians 4: 8-10 Paul says, "*We are troubled on every side, yet not distressed; we are perplexed, but not in despair; Persecuted, but not forsaken; cast down, but not destroy; Persecuted, but not forsaken; cast down, but not destroyed; Always bearing about in the body the dying of the Lord Jesus, that the life also of Jesus might be made manifest in our mortal flesh.*"

David said in Psalm 66: 8-12, "O bless our God, ye people, and make the voice of his praise to be heard: Which holdeth our soul in life, and suffereth not our feet to be moved. For thou, O God hast proved us: thou hast tried us, as silver is tried. Thou broughtest us into the net; thou laidst affliction upon our loins. Thou hast cause men to ride over our heads; we went through fire and through water: but thou broughtest us out into a wealthy place."

LEVEL 5

DEEPER UNDERSTANDING IN HIM

Your accessibility in the spirit realm has a greater authority. You are swimming in deeper waters! The glory of God rest upon you wherever you go, your thoughts are fully aligned to the throne room of God and your will is fully submitted to his will (access granted). You can just easily tap in and out, it is when God has tried you and put you through the fire and he can trust you. When you speak God hears and send angels to carry out and move on your behalf. You are licensed in the spiritual realms, you are now sitting and settling in the office that God has called you to work. Jeremiah 1: 5 state; before I formed thee in the belly I knew; and before thou camest forth out of the womb I sanctified thee, and I ordained thee a prophet unto the nation. Who are you in God and what has he called you to do in his kingdom?

We as believers have to understand and know that God is a God of order. Sometimes he will break his rules to bless someone, he does what pleases him because he is Jehovah. This level takes commitment, submission and consecration. It depends on who God has called you to be, many are called but few are chosen. Some are called for a special purpose and some for a common purpose.

2 Timothy 1:9 says, "Who hath saved us, and called us with an holy calling, not according to our works, but according to his

own purpose and grace, which was given us in Christ Jesus before the world began." You can be in the church for years and still in the same place where you started out. There is no growth and no commitment to nothing, you are spiritual stunted, and stagnant.

Let's look back at John 5, there was a **certain** pool at Bethesda and there was a **certain** man who had an infirmity for thirty and eight years. At a **certain** season angels would come and trouble the water. People got healed when they go in the pool whenever it was troubled by the angel, and for thirty and eight years this man was in the **same** situation, he was right where miracles was taking place but in the same situation. There are people in the church that are in the **same** condition for many years yet no change. The man at the pool of Bethesda had a situation that sounds so familiar, there are so many saints who are in a situation and they keep on going to church pressing and hoping that one day the situation will turn around. He could have asked someone to take him away from the pool or put him in the water.

There are times in our lives when we need a helping hand but we have to open up our mouth and ask for help. Jesus, who is so merciful stopped by that season and said, *will thou be made whole.* The impotent man answered him, *sir I have no one when the water is trouble to put me in the pool.* Here is the Miracle Worker standing before him asking do you want to get out of your situation you're in and he is ready to blame the people around him! Does this sound familiar? There are times when our miracle is there and we get so caught up blaming other people, crying, running, jumping and speaking in tongues, but we did not stop to listen or discern what God wants to do. We missed our breakthrough and our deliverance. Don't get caught up in your emotions and the conditions of your situation lest you miss your season and your breakthrough. When the glory of God shows up, he comes to do something. The churches are full of programs and powerless people, because their lives are not in order. They say yes to God but deny his power, so when God shows up, some church leaders stop the move of the Holy Spirit and proceed with their program. To them, their set agenda is more important than the glory of God. Saints of God, stop, listen and discern! Please stop and discern what the Spirit of the Lord is saying to the church or what he is ready to do. Sometimes we are in an atmosphere that is saturated for healing, deliverance, and breakthrough but the order of service says that it is time for the sermon or the collection of tithes and offering. I am not saying that it is wrong to have order in the church but when God is ready to shift, you must shift! Sometimes the Holy Spirit comes to deposit or download a Rhema in you for ministry but you missed it. Somebody say, "YOU MISSED IT!" Leaders be sensitive to the spirit of the Lord, remember Jesus Christ is the head of the church. God will strengthen you when you are weak or weary.

Revelation 3: 20 Behold, I stand at the door, and knock: if any man hear my voice, and open the door, I will come in to him, and will sup with him, and he with me.

Are we opening the door but not allowing God to do what he wants to do in us and through us? My prayer for us as believers is that we become more sensitive to the Holy Spirit. Be more alert in the realms of the Spirit because it is imperative that we do so. The man who had the infirmity for thirty eight years, said he had no one to put him in the pool when the water was troubled. Yes, sometimes we do need each other Romans 14:7 says," *For none of us liveth to himself, and no man dieth to himself.* Be your brother's keeper."

Ecclesiastes 4:9-12 says, "*Two are better than one; because they have a good reward for their labour. For if they fall, the one will lift up his fellow: but woe to him that is alone when he falleth; for he hath not another to help him up. Again, if two lie together, then they have heat: but how can one be warm alone. And if one prevail against him, two shall withstand him; and a threefold cord is not quickly broken.*" If you're in a situation in dire of help, do you want to come out of your situation? *I am asking you, will thou be made whole?* Jesus said to the man, "Rise, take up thy bed, and walk and instantly he took up his bed and walked." I am asking you again, will thou be made whole? What is it that is holding you captive right now? What is it that has a hold on you? Is it sickness, depression, spirit of rejection, spirit of un-forgiveness, arthritis, a bad relationship, a bad marriage, cult, witchcraft, sexual addiction, pornography, drug addiction, molestation, bitterness, prostitution, fornication, the spirit of fear? You're in church but your bound, wrapped up from the head to the toe like a mummy. Be loosed in the name of Jesus! We know how to fake it; looking good on the outside, all smiling but held captive on the inside. O yes, we know how to dress up the 'sore' pretty good but on the inside it is full of leaking pus. If they could cut us open, they would see that it is not so pretty on the inside. The scripture says man look at the outer appearance but God looks at the heart of man. Jesus came that we may have life and have it more abundantly. He is Jehovah Rapha, he is the Restorer, he is Jehovah Shammah, the God who is always present. He will never leave you nor forsake you even when you are in the midst of a storm he is right there with you in the storm. The storm won't last, just ride out your storm because it will eventually become a "calm". Don't give up because there is light at the end of the tunnel, you have come too far for him to leave you alone.

Hebrews 12: 1-2 says "Wherefore seeing we also are compassed about with so great a cloud of witness, let us lay aside every weight, and the sin which doth so easily beset us, and run with patient the race that is set before us, Looking unto Jesus the author and the finisher of our faith; who for the joy that was set before him endure the cross, despising the shame, and is sit down at the right hand of the throne of God.

LIFT YOUR HANDS AND SAY THIS PRAYER WITH ME

Father I come to you in the name of Jesus and I want to be made whole. You said come unto me all that are heavy laden and I will give you rest so Lord, make me whole. I surrender all to you, heal me Lord Jesus. Wash me and cleanse me from all unrighteousness. Lord make me over, Jesus you endure the cross and despise the shame for me. Lord you paid the price for me at the cross! So by your stripes I am healed. Father deliver me from every situation that has held me captive (call out what has held you in captivity). I speak that by the authority of Jesus Christ that every chains be broken in Jesus name. Father free your sons and daughters in the name of Jesus.

Say… thank you Lord for my healing, thank you Lord that every situation is dried up in Jesus name. Thank you Lord for setting me free from (call it out and make the devil mad because he loves it when you have secrets so he can use it against you) drugs, depression, fornication, prostitution, adultery, arthritis, pornography, bitterness, spirit of fear, envy, malice, witchcraft, sexual addiction, spirit of rejection, soul ties, mental and physical abuse! Father break every chains, bring healing and deliverance in the name of Jesus. If you believe what you prayed give him the glory. Shout HALLELUJAH seven times! Shout from your spirit! Call Jesus! Jesus! Jesus! He hears the cries of his people according to Isaiah 59:1 *"the Lord's hand is not shortened, that it cannot save; neither his ear heavy, that it cannot hear"*, to God be the glory Amen.

Jeremiah 29:11-13 says for I know the thoughts that I think toward you, saith the Lord, thoughts of peace, and not of evil, to give you an expected end. Then shall ye call upon me, and ye shall go and pray unto me, and I will hearken unto you. And ye shall seek me, and find me, when ye shall search for me with all your heart.

Don't only give God your life, but give him your heart. We tend to say Lord I give you my life but our heart is far from him. In Matthew 15:8 *Jesus said to the Scribes and Pharisees, this people draweth nigh unto me with their mouth, and honoureth me with their lips; but their heart is far from me.* Let us examine our self are we giving Jehovah our all, let us not be like the Scribes and the Pharisees.

2 Chronicles 7:13-14 declares" If I shut up heaven that there be no rain, or if I command the locusts to devour the land, or if I send pestilence among my people; If my people, which are called by my name, shall humble themselves, and pray, and seek my face, and turn from their wicked ways; then will I hear from heaven, and will forgive their sin, and will heal their land".

Always remember that the promises of God are sure and without apology or regards to man, but we have to apply ourselves regardless of how we feel about our situation or the oppositions that will come up against us. The oppositions will come, but you have to press your way through it and step into what he has called you to do. Be not afraid because Jehovah is with you even when you can't feel him.

Here are some daily steps that you have to take in order to apply yourself to the will of God:

1. PRESENT YOUR BODY AS A SACRIFICE DAILY,

Romans 12:1-2 *"I beseech you therefore, brethren, by the mercies of God, that ye present your bodies a living sacrifice, holy, acceptable unto God, which is your reasonable service. And be not conformed to this world: but be ye transformed by the renewing of your mind, that ye may prove what is that good, and acceptable, and perfect, will of God"*.

2. BE OBEDIENT TO GOD AND THOSE LEADERS THAT ARE OVER YOU WHO WATCH OUT FOR YOUR SOUL. SUBMIT TO LEADERSHIP.

In Exodus 19:5-6 the Lord God spoke to the children of Israel saying; "Now therefore, if ye will obey my voice indeed, and keep my covenant, then ye shall be a peculiar treasure unto me above all people: for all the earth is mine: And ye shall be unto me a kingdom of priests, and an holy nation. These are the words which thou shalt speak unto the children of Israel." But God did not make Israel a kingdom of priests because of their disobedience.

Jonah was also a perfect example of one who disobeyed God! God told Jonah to go to the great city of Nineveh to cry against it; to warn the people because God said their wickedness has come up before him. In disobedience, Jonah fled from the presence of God and went down to Joppa on a ship. God sent out a great wind into the sea and they cast Jonah off the ship because they were afraid. They knew that they were going to perish so they threw Jonah over board. The bible said the Lord prepared a great fish to swallow up Jonah. For three days and three nights, Jonah repented until God allowed the fish to eject him out of his belly. The bible said Jonah prayed unto the Lord and God who is so merciful spoke unto the fish, and it vomited out Jonah upon the dry land. Then God called Jonah a second time and without any reservation, he arose and did what God told him to do. Many of us are like "modern day-Jonah", but God is a merciful God! He is a God of second chance.

If you are being disobedient to God repent, return to him, cry out to him like Jonah in prayer and he will extend his mercy towards you. It is never too late! There is no situation that God can't take you out of, he is the Sovereign Lord of all. You see, there are people who are waiting for you to reach them, don't let their blood be upon your shoulders.

Isaiah 55:6-7; Seek ye the Lord while he may be found, call ye upon him while he is near: let the wicked forsake his way, and let him return onto the Lord, and he will have mercy upon him; and to our God, for he will abundantly pardon.

Ezekiel 33:6 MSG; But if the watchman sees war coming and, doesn't blow the trumpet, warning the people, I'll hold the watchman responsible for the bloodshed of any unwarned sinner'. I am sure that you would not want any one's blood to be on your shoulders. Jesus is calling you, what are you going to do? Jesus is at the door of your heart knocking, what are you waiting on to let him in? Are you going to allow him to do his work in you and through you? You are a promise and a possibility, no matter who you are God is no respecter of person or nationality.

3. READ THE WORD OF GOD DAILY; STUDY TO SHOW THY SELF-APPROVE;

1 Timothy 4:12- 13 says, "Let no man despise thy youth; but be thou an example of the believers, in word, in conversation, in charity, in spirit, in faith, in purity. Till I come, give attendance to reading, to exhortation, to doctrine. All these thing emulates from you through empowering yourself by reading the word of God."

In Hebrews 4:12, the Bible says, "for the word of God is quick, and powerful, and shaper than any two-edged sword, piercing even to the dividing asunder of soul and spirit, and of the joints and marrow, and is a discerner of the thoughts and intents of the heart".

The word is your weapon against the enemy. In the book of Luke Chapter 4, when Jesus was tempted by the devil; Jesus answered him with the word. He said, "It is written man shall not live by bread alone but by every word of God". He used the Word and he is the word. If the word works for him, (who is the

WORD) I am positive it has to work for us, so work the Word and it will work for you.

4. BE CONSISTENT IN PRAYER AND FASTING;

Let your daily prayer life consists of repentance and thanksgiving. Be disciplined in your fasting, and meditate on the word of God. Also, refrain from watching TV and any other habits that will draw you away from the presence of the Lord in that period of your fasting.

Isaiah 58:6-10 reads, "Is not this the fast that I have chosen? To loose the bands of wickedness, to undo the heavy burdens, and to let oppressed go free, and that ye break every yoke? Is it not to deal thy bread to the hungry, and that thou bring the poor that are cast out to thy house? when thou seest the naked, that thou cover him; and that thou hide not thyself from thine own flesh? Then shall thy light break forth as the morning, and thine health shall spring forth speedily: and thy righteousness shall go before thee; the glory of the Lord shall be thy reward. Then shall thou call and the Lord shall answer; thou shalt cry, and he shall say here I am. If thou take away from the midst of thee the yoke, the putting forth of the finger, and speaking vanity; and if thou draw out thy soul to the hungry, and satisfy the afflicted soul; then shall thy light rise in obscurity and thy darkness be as the noonday".

5. BE PATIENT AND WAIT ON THE LORD FOR INSTRUCTION.

There is a time and season for everything, let us be patient and let God instruct us.

In **Romans: 12:12** the word of God says, "Rejoice in hope; patient in tribulation; continuing instant in prayer".

In **Ecclesiastes** 7:7 it is written, "better is the end of a thing than beginning thereof: and the patient in spirit is better than the proud in spirit.

Psalm 40: 1 – 2 declares, "I waited patiently for the Lord; And he inclined unto me, and heard my cry. He brought me up also out of a horrible pit, out of the miry clay, and set my feet upon a rock, and established my goings".

That is what happens when we wait on the Lord we gain not lose. Seek him for instructions and he will lead you.

In Psalms 23, David says" he leadeth me beside the still waters, he leadeth me in the path of righteousness for is name's sake." He will lead you where he wants you to go! Do not fight the hands of God! He will lead you in green pastures, and hold you up with his right hand. All you have to do is follow him. Sometimes you are disobedient and because of your disobedience, you detour from your purpose. If you repent and surrender before God, he will re-route you to the right path. He is your navigational system. He is the way the truth and the light, let him be a lamp unto your feet and a light unto your path. He said If my people, which are called by my name, shall humble themselves, and pray, and seek my face, and turn from their wicked ways; then will I hear from heaven, and will forgive their sin, and will heal their land. Let go your will so that his will be done in you and through you! After all, we are born for a purpose, his purpose. The scripture says that the enemy is like a roaring lion seeking who he may devour. Put the devil under your feet! He has lost his seat from a long time ago, he is the prince of the air! He has no authority on earth. God gave you the authority; he said whatsoever you bind on earth shall be bound in heaven, and whatsoever you loose on earth will be loose in heaven. When earth moves, heaven respond.

I pray that you will use the authority that God has given you in the earth so that heaven may respond to what you speak. Life and death is in the power of the tongue; the words you speak take form so be very careful what comes out of your mouth. Be careful about the words that you speak over your children. Do not call them using derogatory words instead of their names. In James Chapter 3, the writer talks about the tongue, verse 5 -10 says, "the tongue is a little member, and boasteth great things. Behold how great a matter a little fire kindleth! And the tongue is a fire, a world of iniquity: so is the tongue among our member, that it defile the whole body, and setteth on fire the course of nature; and it is set on fire of hell. For every kind of beasts, and of birds, and of serpent, and of things in the sea, is tamed, and hath been tamed of mankind: But the tongue can no man tame; it is an unruly evil, full of deadly poison. Therewith bless we God, even the Father; and therewith curse we men, which are made after the similitude of God. Out of the same mouth proceedeth blessing and cursing. My brethren, these things ought not so to be." When sickness come upon you, denounce it.

You must speak against the spirit of infirmity. Command it to leave your body because healing is the children's bread, and by his stripes you are healed." Jesus paid the price for us all on Calvary's cross. People tend to receive sickness in their body by owning it (example: **my** arthritis is acting up on me). When you say, "**my, my, my'**, it means that you are already receiving the sickness/disease. When you start owning the sickness, it's difficult to let it go! Command that spirit to leave your body in the name of Jesus. You cannot get healing when you hold on to the infirmity and claim it as your asset. When you own a sickness/disease by adding '**my'** to it, you have already welcomed that disease into your body. Your body is the temple of the Holy Ghost, God lives on the inside of you! Sickness must not dwell in the temple where the Holy Ghost lives. Life and death is in the power of the tongue! You have the same resurrection power that is in Christ Jesus living inside of you, your faith will make you whole.

UNITY IN THE BODY OF CHRIST
ONE BODY ONE GOD ONE SPIRIT

Paul the Apostle of Jesus Christ charged the Corinthians to speak the same mind.

In 1 Corinthians 1:10 (MSG version) Paul said," I have a serious concern to bring up with you, my friend, using the authority of Jesus, our master. I'II put it as urgently as I can: you must get along with each other. You must learn to be considerate of one another, cultivating a life in common."

The Apostle Paul beseeched the brethren to be united together and avoid contentions with one another. He admonished them that there should be no divisions among them. He also entreated them to be perfectly joined together in the same mind and in the same judgement because Christ is not divided. It was not Paul that went to the cross for their sins! They were not baptized in name of Paul but rather in the name of Jesus. Therefore, the Lord wants us (as the body of Christ) to be united in body, and in spirit.

"Now I beseech you, in the name of our Lord Jesus Christ, that ye all speak the same thing, and that there be no divisions among you but that you be perfectly jointed together in the same mind and in the same judgment. For it hath been declared unto me of you, my brethren, by them which are of the house of Chloe, that there are contentions among you. Now this I say, that every one of you saith,

I am of Paul; and I of Apollos; and I of Cephas; and I of Christ. Is Christ divided? Was Paul crucified for you? Or were ye baptized in the name of Paul?" (**1 Corinthians 1: 10-13**)

Where there is division there is confusion, and where there is confusion there is disorder, strive, and jealousy. Division among the body of Christ, open doors and leads all different type of spirit to come in and in so doing, blocks the spirit of the Lord from flowing in full capacity. The Bible says that God is not the author of confusion and discard is not of God but it is of the flesh. David caught the vision in Psalm 133:1-3 and said," Behold, how good and how pleasant it is for brethren to dwell together in unity! It is like the precious ointment upon the head, that ran down upon the beard, even Aaron's beard: that went down to the skirt of his garment; As the dew of Hermon, and as the dew that descended upon the mountain of Zion: for the Lord commanded the blessing, even life for evermore. Blessing cannot flow in confusion and disunity, God does not bless mess, he is a God of order and if the head is not right the blessing can't flow." Ecclesiastes 4:9 -12 states that; "two are better than one; because they have a good reward for their labour. For if they fall, the one will lift up his fellow: but woe to him that is alone when he falleth; for he hath not another to help him up. Again, if two lie together, then they have heat: but how can one be warm alone? John 13:14-15 If I then, your Lord and master, have washed your feet; ye also ought to wash one another's feet. For I have given you an example that ye should do as I have done to you."

AMOS 3:3 CAN TWO WALK TOGETHER, EXCEPT THEY BE AGREED?

When there is unity in the body of Christ, we become one, and the enemy has no entrance way to step into our lives! Do not give the enemy access or permission to gain entry into your life because of disunity. Unity does not mean that we do not have different opinions or different personalities, we can be united but there are differences in the natural or physical aspect of our lives. We are entitled to our own opinions, but any decisions made in ministry or in the church, must be done to the glory of God. When all is said and done, it is not about you but it's about God's will for you, our spiritual growth, and building the kingdom of God. Jesus said, I and the Father are one. He did not do anything out of the will of his Father because they are one. So why are churches divided and the members not on one accord? Why do the members want to tell the leaders what to do or how to preach? There are protocols that the church must adhere to, and obedience is better than sacrifice. Unity spells loyalty! God used Moses to deliver his people out of Egypt. He led them through the wilderness but God did not use him to bring them into the promise land. He used Joshua to lead them instead. When saints walk with God, they have made a covenant with him. You cannot make a covenant if there are disagreements, the TWO HAVE TO AGREE. Agreements are made when there is evidence of faith on both sides.

There is a time and season for everything. Sometimes God will replace some people to prepare them for his next move. But sometimes it can cause a lot of problem in the church because some people are resistant to change, while there are others who are ready to accept the change. God will raise up the faithful and obedient ones and move them in a different position where they can grow spiritually and flourish in grace. Some will feel as if they are rejected when not given the opportunity to work in the house of the Lord. These are the same people who will oppose to leadership because of the spirit of antagonism and rebellion. They will begin to sow discord among the brethren or they may even leave the church. This negative behavior should not among the true blood-washed saints of God. Walking together in unity and agreement will catapult you into your divine destiny. We have a mandate! We have a task to perform! We must go out to all parts of the earth and win souls for Christ for united we stand but divided we fall. Stand tall for God! Walk in love and agreement.

In Ephesians 4:1-8, Paul the Apostle of Jesus Christ appealed to the people saying," I therefore, the prisoner of the Lord, beseech you that ye walk worthy of the vocation wherewith ye are called, With all lowliness and meekness, with longsuffering, forbearing one another in love; Endeavouring to keep the unity of the Spirit in the bond of peace. There is one BODY, and one SPIRIT, even as ye are called in one hope of your calling; One LORD, one FAITH, one BAPTISM, one GOD and Father of all, who is above all, and through all, and in you all. But unto every one of us is given grace according to the measure of the gift of Christ. In verse 11-16 of the same chapter, the Bible said, "And he gave some, Apostles; and some, prophets; and some, Evangelists; and some, Pastors and teachers; For the perfecting of the saints, for the work of the ministry, for the edifying of the body of Christ: Till we all come in the unity of the faith, and of the knowledge of the son of God, unto a perfect man, unto the measure of the stature of the fullness of Christ: That we henceforth be no more children, tossed to and fro, and carried about with every wind of doctrine, by the sleight of men, and cunning craftiness, whereby they lie in wait to deceive; But speaking the truth in love, may grow up into him in all things, which is the head, even Christ: From whom the body fitly joined together and compacted by that which every joint supplieth, according to the effectual working in the measure of every part, maketh increase of the body unto the edifying of itself in love."

PARTS OF THE HUMAN BODY

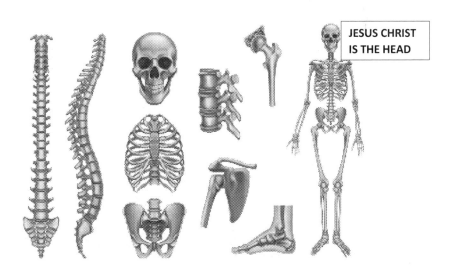

JESUS CHRIST
IS THE HEAD

We are one body, (this diagram is just an example of how we are one body in Christ Jesus) and when we unite together, we become a whole. But if the parts detach themselves from their respective position the body will eventually fall apart. If the head is separated from the rest of the body, there would be no direction, no instruction and no leadership because it is the brain (which sits in the cranium, inside the head that sends out the signal to the rest of the body and instruct them when to move, how to move, and where to move. Without HEAD OF THE CHURCH (Jehovah God), there is no source of life, no eternal life, no light and no guide.

The body of Christ is made up of many members but we are one body. Just as your natural body that is made up of different body parts that are connected together; your hands, your feet, your eyes, fingers and toes; each part has a purpose and a specific function to perform. If you lose your eyes you cannot see, if you lose your feet you cannot walk. You are considered disabled because you will no longer be able to function effectively. Yet, there are people that are disabled but they are not hindered from performing the same roles as those who are abled. Their lack does not stand in the way or prevent them from doing the things they want to do. Physical disability does not always means incapability. Sometimes these are the very ones that God will use bless your soul. Likewise, the body of Christ needs to function as many members in one body, united as one, embrace one another's ministry and gifts, exhort one another in unity, because we are joined together in Christ Jesus our Savior.

In 1 Corinthians 12: 20-27, the scripture said," But now are they many member, yet but one body. And the eye cannot say unto the hand, I have no need of thee: nor again the head to the feet, I have no need of you. Nay, much more those members of the body, which seem to be more feeble, are necessary: And those members of the body, which we think to be, less honorable, upon these we bestow more abundant honor; and uncomely parts have more abundant comeliness. For our comely parts have no need: but God hath tempered the body together, having given more abundant honor to that part which lacked: That there should be no schism in the body; but that the members should have the same care one for another. And whether one member suffer, all the members suffer with it; or one member be honored, all the members rejoice with it. Now ye are the body of Christ, and members in particular".

For it is God which worketh in you both to will and to do of his good pleasure (Philippians 2:13). One can chase a thousand and two ten thousand to flight.

WE ARE ONE SPIRIT

In Acts 2:1- 6; the Bible says, "And when the day of Pentecost was fully come, they were all with one accord in one place. And suddenly there came a sound from heaven as of a rushing mighty wind, and it filled all the house where they were sitting. And there appeared unto them cloven tongues like as of fire, and it sat upon each of them. And they were filled with the Holy Ghost, and began to speak with other tongues, as the Spirit gave them utterance." We are amazed to see and witness the miracles and awesomeness of God! If we will come together in the spirit, what miraculous things that could be done by the power of the Holy Spirit! Only if the people of God would just lay aside everything that so easily beset them, because we wrestle not against flesh and blood but against principalities and power and the rulers of darkness and spiritual wickedness in high places.

ONE LORD

Jesus Christ is Lord over all. There is one body, and one Spirit, even as ye are called in one hope of your calling; **one Lord**, one Faith, one baptism" (Ephesians 4:4-5). The Bible says in Philippians 2:8-11 that Jesus came fashioned as a man, he humbled himself, and become obedient unto death, even the death of the cross. Wherefore God also hath highly exalted him, and given him a name which is above every name: that at the name of Jesus every knee should bow, of things in heaven, and things in the earth, and things under the earth; And that every tongue should confess that Jesus Christ is Lord, to the glory of God the Father.

ONE FAITH

We have confidence to believe that God is able to do exceedingly abundantly all we can even ask or think. *"For the vision is yet for an appointed time, but at the end it shall speak, and not lie: though it tarry, wait for it; because it will sure come, it will not tarry. Behold, his soul which is lifted up is not upright in him: but the Just shall live by his faith."* (Habakkuk 2:3-4) Salvation is a faith walk with God not knowing what's going to happen. It is a walk where you just go as long as God is leading you and having the faith to know that he will come through for you if you trust him. Faith is the substance of things hope for and the evidence of things not seen. In Mark 11:22 Jesus saith unto his disciple, *"Have faith in God. For verily I say unto you that whosoever shall say unto this mountain, be thou removed, and be cast into the sea; and shall not doubt in his heart, but shall believe that those things which he saith shall come to pass; he shall have whatsoever he saith. Therefore I say unto you, what things soever ye desire, when ye pray, believe that ye receive them, and ye shall have them."*

"One faith" also refers to all the beliefs and practices Christians take from the Word and Spirit of God. There is only one faith, this "one faith" is the very heart of the gospel, for it is the power of God to them that believe (Romans 1:16-17).

Back in Ephesians 4, Paul goes on to write "till we all come to the unity of the faith" (v. 13), conceding that Christians had not yet come to perfect unity in all aspect of the one faith. Without this faith it is impossible to please God, because he that cometh to God must believe that he is a rewarder to them that diligently seek him.

ONE GOD AND FATHER OF ALL.

In the beginning God created the heaven and the earth. Before the beginning, he was God before the foundation of the world was laid, he was and is still the father of all. In Exodus Chapter 3 when God appeared to Moses in the burning bush, he identified himself to Moses and said I am the God of thy father, the God of Abraham, the God of Isaac, and the God of Jacob, I AM THAT I AM! God, the Father can be anything you want him to be. He is versatile like that! Nobody is greater than the Creator, the Father of all. He is God all by himself, give him the glory and all the honor, Amen.

REPENTANCE

Repentance is a summons to a personal, absolute and ultimate unconditional surrender to God as Sovereign. It includes sorrow and regrets when you sin against God, and you ask him for forgiveness and mercy. It is the turning away from and sin, and turning to God. In repenting, one makes a complete change of direction and move towards God. Repentance means to be remorseful for any sinful action that causes you to sin against

God, and asking him to forgive you and have mercy. It is a turning around from sin and turn to God. As Christians, it is important to let our daily prayers unto God include repentance. This is the first step after acknowledging who you are. Praying to and exaltation unto him repentance should be the next step because all have sinned and come short of the glory of God.

1 John 1: 8-10 "if we say that we have no sin, we deceive ourselves, and the truth is not in us. If we confess our sins, he is faithful and just to forgive us our sins, and to cleanse us from all unrighteousness. If we say that we have not sinned, we make him a liar, and his word is not in us".

Let God be true and every man a liar, we all have sinned and come short of the glory of God. Don't let your mistakes or sins keep you bound, confess and move on because God is merciful towards us and he is a forgiving God. Don't be presumptuous before God, although he is merciful; he is also a God of judgment and he will punish you as he see it fit. Romans 3:23 says, "For all have sinned, and come short of the glory of God." Be real to yourself; God already knows us and he knows what we are capable of doing, he made man and he is God.

A perfect example of repentance is shown when King David, in 2 Samuel chapter 11 and 12, sinned against God and slept with Uriah's wife Bath-Sheba. God sent Nathan the prophet to confront King David about his sin. Sometimes you're so deep in sin that it feels so good. You get so familiar and acclimatized to doing **wrong** until they feel like they are **right.** David went as far as to commit murder, but he did not do it himself. He gave the orders to cover up his sin. But David was very good at repentance. In Psalm 51:14 he said," Deliver me from bloodguiltiness, O God, thou God of my salvation: and my tongue shall sing aloud of thy righteousness."

As human beings, we have a tendency to make excuses for our sins. We do not exercise accountability for our actions, but God is always watching us, and we cannot hide from him. The Lord is omniscient, he knows everything! He knows the beginning and the end of everything. We cannot surprise the father, all things are naked before him, so David confessed his sins before God. Our merciful God reminded David of the blessings he had given him and told him that there is a penalty for this great sin that he had committed before him. *To whom much is given much is required of you!* You are accountable for your actions even when you repent, God will judge you and punish you for your sins. He will do whatever he feels to do. He is God, and he will take away or destroy what was conceived in sin when you turn to him in repentance. God took the child from David that was conceived in his sin. David besought the Lord for the child, he fasted, and went in, and laid all night before the Lord, but God took the child from him (he died).

Repentance is necessary for your Christian walk. It is turning away from sin and submitting yourself to God, Let us take an

Being On The Inside - The Church In Motion

introspective look on our lives to see if we are in right standing with God. Is there any sin in your life that will cause an open door for the enemy to gain access in your life? Examine yourself now! The scripture says, let a man examine himself. Is there any sin in your life that would cause God to turn his face from you and not hear your prayers? You must repent if you search yourself and find any trace of sin in your heart. 2 Chronicle 7:14 says" If my people, which are called by my name, shall humble themselves, and pray, and seek my face, and turn from their wicked ways; then will I hear from heaven, and will forgive their sin, and will heal their land." Therefore, if the people that are called Christians would acknowledge their sins and repent, and seek the face of God in humility; then God will hear and forgive them of their sins and bring healing to their land, their body, their soul.

Isaiah 6:1-9 stated that, "in the year that king Uzziah died I saw also the Lord sitting upon a throne, high and lifted up, and his train filled the temple. Above it stood the Seraphim's: each one had six wings; with twain he covered his face, and with twain he covered his feet and with twain he did fly. And one cried unto another, and said, Holy, Holy, Holy, is the Lord of hosts: the whole earth is full of his glory. And the posts of the door moved at the voice of him that cried, and the house was filled with smoke. Then said I, Woe is me! For I am undone; because I am a man of unclean lips, and I dwell in the midst of a people of unclean lips: for mine eyes have seen the king, the Lord of hosts.

Then flew one of the seraphim's unto me, having a live coal in his hand, which he had taken with the tongs from off the altar: And he laid it upon my mouth, and said, lo, this hath touched thy lips; and thine iniquity is taken away, and thy sin purged. Also I heard the voice of the Lord, saying, whom shall I send, and who will go for us? Then said I, here am I; send me. And he said, Go, and tell this people, hear ye indeed, but understand not; and see ye indeed, but perceive not." Isaiah admitted that he was not worthy to be in the presence of the Lord, then the angel of the Lord took a live coal and placed it upon Isaiah's mouth and took away his iniquity and purged him. When you allow God to purge you, you will be fit for the Master's use.

You might be saying Lord, I have some struggles and I am in the midst of bad company or friends! Or, you may even say, I am living with a man or woman that I am not married to, my life is a mess! Lord, I am not in the place that you would want me to be, my garment is wrinkled! You have acknowledged that you have sinned when you reach the point and begin to say, "Lord am a sinful man or woman, I am not worthy, Lord use someone else". You may not even realize that you are the one God wants to use. God knows that you cannot do nothing in your own strength, but he will allow you to go through the process so that he can get the glory. Jesus disciples was a perfect example, they weren't highly educated men but God is not like man. God looks for a broken heart and a contrite spirit but man qualifies you based on intellectual potentials and college degrees. God will pick up the drug dealer, the prostitute, a drug addict, a lawyer or doctor and convert them into fishers of men and to declare his word.

"Behold, the Lord's hand is not shortened, that it cannot save; neither his ear heavy that it cannot hear: But your iniquity have separated between you and your God, and your sins have hid his face from you, that he will not hear." (Isaiah 59: 1-2)

God can reach you whether you are in the darkest part of hell or in the miry clay. He took Joseph from the pit to the palace. Hebrews 4:16 says, "Let us therefore come boldly unto the throne of grace that we may obtain mercy, and find grace to help in time of need." Repentance is a sincere act, straight from the heart. Admitting that you are wrong is the first step to obtain forgiveness. Don't let your pride or disobedience pull you away from God! If you are not in the presence of the Lord, you are in the path of his Judgment and God is no respecter of a person. REPENT IF YOU SINNED AND FALLEN SHORT OF GOD'S GLORY! It is appointed unto men once to die, but after this the Judgment (Hebrews 9: 27). There is no repentance in the grave. As long as you are in the land of the living, you have a chance to repent and get back into the presence of the Lord. Sin will cause God to turn his face from you. If you do not repent you will not escape his judgment, the judgment of God is sure to the children of disobedience. Beloved I beseech you that you walk in obedience and have a repentant heart towards God. He is the one that you have sinned against.

David says it best in Psalm 51: 1- 19 says" Have mercy upon me, o God, according to thy lovingkindness: according unto the multitude of thy tender mercies blot out my transgressions. Wash me thoroughly from mine iniquity, and cleanse me from my sin. For I acknowledge my transgressions: and my sin is ever before me. Against thee only, have I sinned, and done this evil in thy sight: that thou mightiest be justified when thou speakest, and be clear when thou judgest. Behold, I was shapen in inquity; and in sin did my mother conceive me. Behold, thou desirest truth in the inward parts: and in the hidden part thou shalt make me to know wisdom. Purge me with hyssop, and I shall be clean: wash me, and I shall be whiter than snow. Make me to hear joy and gladness; that the bones which thou hast broken may rejoice. Hide thy face from my sins, and blot out all mine iniquities. Create in me a clean heart, O God; and renew a right spirit within me. Restore unto me the joy of thy salvation; and uphold me with thy free spirit. Then will I teach transgressors thy ways; and sinners shall be converted unto thee. Deliver me from bloodguiltiness, O God, thou God of my salvation: and my tongue shall sing aloud of thy righteousness. O Lord, open thou my lips; and my mouth shall shew forth thy praise. For thou desirest not sacrifice; else would I give it: thou delightest not in burnt offering. The sacrifices of God are a broken spirit: A broken and contrite heart, O God, thou wilt not despise. Do good in thy good pleasure unto zion: build thou the walls of Jerusalem. Then shalt thou be pleased with the sacrifice of righteousness, with burnt offering and whole burnt offering: then shall they offer bullocks upon thine altar".

We saw in Psalms 51 that David first step to repentance was to ask God for mercy, then he asked God to wash away his iniquity and cleanse him from his sins. He said," I acknowledge my transgressions." David admitted to his mistakes, his sins, his transgressions against God, he humbled himself before the Lord, he was broken before him. The sacrifice of God are a broken and contrite heart, God will not despise. God will not reject your pleas when you come before him broken, remorseful, sorrowful, and feel genuinely sorry for the sins that you committed against him. Some of us often take God for granted. We keep on doing the same thing over and over and ask him to forgive us of the same sin. Paul said in Romans 6: 1, "shall we say then? What shall we continue to sin, that grace may abound". Shall we continue to take advantage of the grace and mercy of God? God wants us to live a holy life a life that is pleasing unto him. Paul wrote in Romans 12: 1-2," I beseech you therefore, brethren, by the mercies of God that ye present your bodies a living sacrifice, holy, acceptable unto God, which is your reasonable service. And be not conformed to this world: but be ye transformed by the renewing of your mind, that ye may prove what is that good, and acceptable, and perfect, will of God."

But as he which hath called you is holy, so be ye holy in all manner of conversation; because it is written, Be ye holy; for I am holy (1 Peter 1:15-16)

We are obligated to do what is right when we say YES to Christ Jesus; we have to be accountable to God for our behavior. Walk in the spirit so you won't desire the lust of the flesh. Galatians 5:16-21," this I say then, walk in the spirit, and ye shall not fulfill the lust of the flesh. For the flesh lusteth against the spirit, and the spirit against the flesh: and these are contrary the one to the other: so that ye cannot do the things that ye would. But if ye be led of the spirit, ye are not under the law. Now the work of the flesh are manifest, which are these; Adultery, fornication, uncleanness, lasciviousness, Idolatry, witchcraft, hatred, variance, emulations, wrath, strife, seditions, heresies, envy, murders, drunkenness, revellings, and such like: of the which I tell you before, as I have also told you in time past, that they which do such things shall not inherit the kingdom of God."

In Titus 2:11-13, the Word of God says," For the grace of God that bringeth salvation hath appeared to all men, teaching us that, denying ungodliness and worldly lusts, we should live soberly, righteously, and Godly, in this present world; looking for that blessed hope, and the glorious appearing of the great God and our savior Jesus Christ; who gave himself for us, that he might redeem us from all iniquity, and purify unto himself a peculiar people, zealous of good works."

Sin will keep you in bondage and disconnect you from God. *You may ask, how can sin keep me in bondage?* Sin can become a barrier between you and God, it is a hindrance to your spiritual walk with God. Sin will also cause you to miss your season and you don't know how long you have to wait before the season comes back! So children of God; repent and walk in the righteousness of God! Proverbs 14: 34 states that," Righteousness exalteth a nation: but sin is a reproach to any people." In the book of Psalms 5:12, David wrote, "for thou, Lord, wilt bless the righteous; with favor wilt thou compass him as with a shield. Let your desire be that your walk holy before God and man he said to shine your light that man may see so he may be glorified." I charge you as saints of God, do not let your flesh have power over you, take authority over it! You are more than conqueror in Jesus Christ. We are infused with power from on high through Jesus Christ.

HOW GOD CAN TAKE PEOPLE OUT OF OBSCURITY AND USE THEM AS VESSEL OF HONOR FOR HIS GLORY

I was born and raised in Kingston Jamaica West Indies. I am the third child of four siblings on my mother side of the family. My mom was a single parent whose role was to take care of her kids, without the help of a mate. As a dressmaker (seamstress), she worked very hard to make ends meet and to put food on the table. She was a strong woman who made sure we had clothes on our back and shoes on our feet. Though she struggled, she gave us the best she had or what she could afford. It was evident that she cared and loved us dearly. We didn't have much but we did not allow our limitations to define us. We were involved in so many activities which included participating in national and cultural festivals, and girl's scout. It was customary for my mom to drop us off at church on Saturdays or Sundays each week. Church was like a kind of daycare for us because she would get the time to do certain chores in order to put provide food for us. When I was nine years old, my mom got very ill. She had no prior illness, but she died within a few days. Her death was so sudden and we took it real hard. My sister who was just a year old at the time also took sick at the same time and died a few days after. She too, had no prior illness either both of them each died within days of each other. It was painful at the time, I just could not understand what was happening to me. My family structured changed in a flash of time and I was in a state of shock. I was left all alone abandon with no one to call parents. My older sister was about to start high school, but there was no parental guidance for us. After a while we were located to a 'tenement yard', a living place ;pretty much like a building complex. I was left alone for a little while at the age of nine. One day my oldest sister came to the house and when she saw me, she asked why I was left by myself.

We had to go to friends' houses to sleep on their floor at nights. Each night we would sleep on the floor of a different house. We finally went back to the house where my mom was living. My aunt who is my mother's sister came looking for me. At that time she was living in a different place on the country side (far from where I was living). My grandfather had sent her to get me to come and live with him. May God bless his soul, he passed away at the age of ninety-eight). I remembered my granddad as a God fearing man. He was always talking to God on his family's behalf. I remembered how much he loved me. It was a special love that only a true grandfather could give. My granddad sat down with me on the day of my mother's funeral. He looked me in the eyes and he told me said, *"Leonie, the stone that the builder rejected shall be the head corner stone."* He took me in and send me to school. His only occupation was that he was a butcher (someone who killed cows, and goats and sold the meat at the market). He did not have a lot of money, but he did what he could with what he had and we never complained. We were blessed!

My Grandfather was a man of great faith. I would hear him at night praying straight through the night. His routine was to go to bed early and then wake up and talk to God all throughout the night. But I had an aunt that would complain in the morning that she could not sleep because he was too disruptive all through the night. He would pray and then stop in between to have conversations with God. I would often hear him speaking aloud about his kids and grandkids. As a child, I always wondered how he got his rest at nights. At times I would go to school without lunch money because my grandad had none to give. I would walk for two miles to get to school, it was humbling for me and I did not complain. The good part was that I literally loved school. Many other kids in my neighborhood were walking home as well. We automatically walked together as a group. We would have fun walking there together in cane fields on both side of the road. The habit of stopping to eat sugar cane became a daily routine. As kids, we were contented with what we had and what we have to do to survive. In this age and time, children have so much privileges and opportunities in life. Some of them are given more than they can even manage. When my mom died, one of my sister could not attend her funeral. At that time, she was only 12 years old and living with her dad (under strict parental control). I carried that burden with me for many years. I felt bad that she did not get to pay her last respect, it saddened my heart. For years I thought about her, where she was, and what she was doing.

Back in Jamaica, I used to listen a radio program that was aired every Sunday called" **Sunday Contact**" This program was like a life saver to those who lost touch with their love ones or friends, they could send written letters to the program, and the host would read the letter on the air. One Sunday while I was listening to the program, something began to stir up on the inside of me. It was like an inner voice telling me that I should write a letter to find my sister that I have not seen for years. I obeyed that compelling demand and wrote a letter and send it to **Sunday Contact to be read.** I kept this thought from my guardian (grandfather) and cousins that I was living with, no one knew about it. My aunt's radio was the only radio in the house and so I could only listen the program when she was home. My letter was read the day when I did not get opportunity to listen to Sunday Contact. This was because my aunt wasn't at home and that's when the host happened to read my letter on the air. I found out that a friend of the family heard when it was read, and wrote down the information. Back then, cell phones or house phones were not popular and so the only mode of contacting people was by using their address. The next thing I knew was that, shortly afterwards, someone informed me that my letter was read on the radio.

I had just started high school and was on the morning shift; this means that my school starts at 8am and ended precisely at 12 noon. Back then in Jamaica, the school's population in most schools had two shifts; morning and afternoon, due to the fact that the population of students were too large. One afternoon when I got home from school, my grandfather said to me," Leonie, someone is here to see you!" By this time my grandad had already heard about the letter I sent to the radio station. I found out that a family member from my dad's side came to visit and was planning for me to live with her. When I left my grandfather's house, I was held against my own will. My 'new' guardian never gave me permission to visit my grandfather's house, the place where I used to live! Two years had passed since I left, and truly I missed my grandfather. I felt homesick because I wanted to see him. My guardian gave me an ultimatum either I go to visit him and don't come back or I stay with them, so I chose to visit him.

My family structure changed to one where I went to live in the city (Kingston) with my sister, brother, and biological father. My father later migrated to the United States and left us back in Jamaica. I spoke to him on the phone but I was silently angry with the fact that if he had been in my life age, I wouldn't have gone through so much in my formative years (age of nine). I had so many questions that I needed answers. I carried that bitterness with me for years, and the spirit of rejection captivated my heart. Years after I migrated to the USA. I ended up in a verbal and physical abusive relationship that was mistaken for love. I stayed in relationships because I did not want to be alone, not realizing that I was searching for love in the wrong places. The devil had me bound, I was attracted to the wrong people. I used to feel like I was never good enough for anyone. I felt I like I was not worthy to be loved and my self-esteem was rock-bottom low. When people gave me compliments like, "you are a pretty young girl!" I would casually say, "thank you," but I never believed.

If you find yourself in an abusive relationship or marriage, whether physically or verbally abused, I want you to know that you deserve better. It is not emotionally-healthy to grow up witnessing your mom been abused by her spouse, and later find yourself living in an abusive relationship and remained silent about it. You cannot be complacent or misinterpret what you are getting as true love! Don't mind the stigma that goes with it, don't be ashamed to talk about it! Be free in the name of Jesus!

If you are still in an abusive relationship right now, walk out! Don't be complacent! Don't worry about what people may say about you. Jesus came that you may have abundant life, do not settle for less, you deserve the best life in abundance. John 10:10 says," The thief cometh not, but for to steal, and to kill, and to destroy: I am come that they might have life, and that they might have it more abundantly". At one point in my life, I was in a long standing relationship that was not working well. I was afraid to walk away from the relationship because I thought that loneliness would have tormented me. I was worried about what people were going to say about me. If you have children you may feel like you cannot raise them by yourself, or that you will not manage physically and financially, but God will take care of you!

I gave my life to the Lord out of despair, I was left to take care of my two kids all by myself. One song writer said" sometimes it takes a mountain, sometimes a troubled sometimes it takes a desert to get a hold of me" Today I can testify that if we open our heart to God, he will do the rest for us. Growing up during my childhood days, I knew that there was something peculiar about me because I would have dreams about something and I would see it manifest before my eyes. But, I did not understand that it was a gift from God. When I was young, my cousins and I had to go to church even if we did not want to go. I was going but I did not recognize the calling of God on my life. When I accepted the Lord as my personal Savior, I would often cry and say, Lord how am I going to raise these two children by myself?" My daughter was three years old and my son was about six years old, I had no family member around and I was petrified. I remembered crying one night and I heard a voice said" ***it's not by might nor by power but by my spirit***!" That moment, I stopped crying and began to depend on Jesus. The Lord took me in, I became a part of his royal family! A joint-heir with Jesus! He became my Savior, my Protector, my Friend, my Father, my Deliverer, my Help. Today, I give him thanks and praise because he never leave me nor forsake me, when I am out of his order he corrects me, he chastise me, and I give him the glory because he is a good, good Daddy to me.

I can tell you this; I truly love the Lord and I teach my children to have a heart after God. My children are at the age now where they understand who God is. I remember coming from church one night and the anointing was upon me very strongly, I was speaking to them about God. I said to my son, "I know you love me, but love God more", my kids were silent when they heard what I said. A couple of weeks after that, we were on our way home and my son said to me," mom you said I should love God more than you but isn't God in you?" When you live a life that is pleasing to God, your children will see the light in you; they are watching you! Be an example to your children. If I am not feeling well, the first thing my kids would do, especially my daughter, would come and lay her hands on me and pray that God would heal me, I thank God for them. My walk with God has been a struggle at times; the persecution, the ridicule was not in vain.

They may hate you for the cause of Christ, but hold on. At times, I would complaining to God and ask, "Why people don't like me? Why do they just curse me out without a cause?" When there is purpose on your life, God will allow you to be in certain situations to try you and work on you. It's not a good feeling, but when you go through the fire, his glory will be revealed in you. In the end, when God is through with you, you will come out as pure gold. Some people walk away because of the process, some will stand up as willing soldiers. If you are going through testing, be of good courage! Be strong in the Lord and in the power of his might! Your future is secure in God! Don't give up on God, he will not give up on you!

I have made a lot of mistakes but I get back up and moved on because of the grace of God. Don't feel condemned when you mess up, it does not surprise God. He knows that you were going to mess up in the first place. Repent and move on! In the churches today, people tend to quickly put a label on others when they slip, and if the truth be told, they too have skeletons in their closet. Peter Tosh a Jamaican reggae artist, sang a song, the lyrics states that *if you live in a glass house don't through stone.* I thank God for the blood that washes and cleanse us from all unrighteousness. Let us be our brother's keeper, pull them up instead of pushing the down, because you might be in a situation where someone prayed for you to get back up, amen.

In my walk with God I experienced many difficulties, trials, tribulation, sufferings, and discomfort. I give God thanks for every tumultuous situations that I have been through, because it is in those times I learned to be humble, to seek his face more. I remember been homeless for a couple months, I had nowhere to live. Then someone I knew, introduced me to an old man who lived alone in his house. This old man was also sick. And so the person asked him if he could allow my small family (myself and my two children) to stay there for a while until I could get an apartment for myself. I was happy when he said yes, but that happiness was short-lived. When I went there, the place was in a horrible state; the smell was so unbearable that my son ended up in the hospital with asthma for a couple of days. The odor was difficult to manage, it was horrible to take into my nostrils. I later found out that there were also demonic spirits lurking around in the house at nights.

I remembered one night, a church sister came to visit me at my workplace and dropped me home. As soon has she entered the door and sat down in the living room, she knew that something was wrong. My head grew three times as big and felt as heavy as lead. My church sister began to speak in tongues, as she spoke, she opened the front door and ended up on the porch, still speaking in tongues. I started to pray as well. She later told me that she saw a demon in the form of a woman but, it left the house while she spoke in her heavenly language. After she told me about the demon, I began to tell her about my nightly encounters with these evil spirits that tried to prevent me from sleeping at nights. Each night I had to pray constantly without ceasing. I was afraid at that time because my kids were very young and they did not understand what was going on. Deep within me, I trusted God. I knew somehow that God would never leave me. No one knew what I was going through at nights because I would wear a smile on my face in pretense that everything was alright.

One night God gave me a vision. In my vision, I saw debris on the floor of the porch. The Lord showed me that the man had changed the lock on the door. A few days after, my vision manifested before my eyes. As I was about to opened the door, I realized that the lock was changed and so I stood at the door with my two children. When I rang the doorbell and the little old man came and opened the door. He started to curse me out and said that I must leave his house. I asked if I have done something wrong because of the expression that he had on his face and the tone of his voice, but he did not answer. I knew that because of his age, sometimes his mind would be thinking strangely-wild and out of line. I did not pay much attention to him regarding his behavior. When I looked in his eyes, it was like I was looking in the eyes of a demon. He was so loud that his neighbors woke up, asking what the commotion was all about. He told me that I should leave his house by the end of the week. I walked passed him without saying a word, and went to the room and gently closed the door behind me. I was instantly shaken up by what happened but after a couple of minutes, I started to speak to God about the situation. I felt bad for my children who witnessed this man cursing at me and showing me such disrespect.

My old landlord was not physically-abled. He was not in a position to do his chores, and so a lady would come two days a week to do housecleaning and laundry for him. When I scarcely scanned the old man's house that was supposedly cleaned house, I was touched by emotions because, cleaning had not yet started. The rooms were in the same condition as if they were not touched by a cleaner. When she went on a leave, I asked the house owner if I could clean his house for him but he said no! He mentioned that he already had someone to get the work done. I later found out that the cleaner lady would take his valuable items and told the man that I was the thief. One morning after I dropped my kids off to school, I silently closed my room door and went back to bed. No one knew that I was in the house. I was really tired and drained from all night prayer. While I was lying there, I heard when someone tried to pull on my door, I remained silent and almost motionless. I could hear when the person moved away from my door and went down the stairs. Then I overheard her conversation with the old man; she asked," *When is she going to leave?*" Obviously her agenda was to plant bad seeds in this man's heart against me. I got up very quietly, without making a sound, got dressed and went down the stairs. I slipped through the door without them even noticing.

When I reached my workplace, I called the lady that sent me to the house. She was a very good friend of the little old man, so I told her what was going on. She told me that she was the one that got the cleaning job for this woman, and that she could not believe that she would have done such a thing. Each time that the lady would come to the house, she would plant a bad seed into the little old man's heart that caused his anger to grow even more against me. When I got home in the evenings and I would say, good evening, but he would just look at me with a mean face and said nothing. Then one day while I was at my workplace, the lady that introduced me to the little old man told me that the cleaner lady's landlord gave her notice and she asked the little old man if she could stay at his house with her family, but he said no. That was when I realized that her agenda was to get rid of me so she could stay at the house. I did not retaliated, I did not confront her, I did not take revenge, but I put my case before God in prayer. The bible said in the book of Ephesian 6:12 that, "we wrestle not against flesh and blood, but against principalities, against powers, against the rulers of the darkness of this world, against spiritual wickedness in high places".

In the back of my mind, I wanted the cleaner woman to know that I knew what she was doing. One morning as I came out of the front door, I saw a man sitting on the steps that led to the doorway. As soon as I got close to him, I told him good morning and left. To make a long story short, the man was her male companion. She would take him to work with her when I was not at home. It was later found out that some money was missing from the old man's house. When he asked her about the money, she told him that she did not know anything about what he was talking about. The old man found out that she was a dishonest person.

One morning when she showed up for work, he chased her out of his house. He fired her and told her that she should not return to his house. He then apologized to me for the way he treated me. From that day, his attitude changed towards me. He quickly evolved into a different person; having good conversations with me. I started to tell him that he needs to give his life over to God. I read bible scriptures with him and told him about God's mercy and his grace. Then one night I was praying about an apartment, I heard the Spirit of the Lord said, *"Before the 24th of next month you are going to get an apartment."* When I heard that, it was like music to my ears. I said thank you Lord because I believe it was so. At that time, it was about the second week in the month of November, and the next month would be December. I began to pray that God would provide me with an apartment before Christmas so that my children would be in their own beds by Christmas day. On the 23rd of November of that year, the Lord answered my prayer and I got an apartment. Someone in my church bought a house and was renting one of the floors, and God favored me. Hallelujah!! My rough years have placed me in a position to be the woman of God that I am today! The Potter was molding me into an intercessor because I was constantly praying and seeking God for myself and others. To God be the glory great things he has done!

No matter what situation you are in right now, just stay before God in prayer and fasting and he will work it out. When you trust in the Lord with all your heart and lean not to your own understanding, he will change your mountain into a plain! He will calm your tempest! He will turn your life around! There is always testimony in your tests and a message from your mess. Stop and pay attention, because the real you will show up in the valley. **The Lily of the Valley** will show up for you! God is a good and he is worthy to be praised. I remember one night when my son was about 7 years old, I was sleeping and the Spirit of the Lord opened my eyes. When I looked, I saw my son standing at my bed side gasping for breath. There was no word coming from his mouth, I was so frightened and in shock. I remembered grabbing him and laying my hand on his chest. His heart was beating so fast as if it would stop beating soon. I started to pray in tongues an in a couple seconds, his heart rate went back to normal and he started to breathe with ease. At that time I did not know that I was an intercessor. I didn't even know who I was in God, and what he has called me to do. Before I came into the knowledge of who I was in the spirit, the spirit of the Lord quickened me. In John 6:63, the Bible says that, *it is the spirit that quickeneth; the flesh profiteth nothing: the words that I speak unto you, they are spirit, and they are life*".

In 2011, I was in prayer one day with two prayer partners when the Spirit of the Lord spoke to me saying," Go to Fleetwood train station!" The next morning at 9am, he said "do not be late, I will have someone there waiting for you." We did not hesitate, we got up early that morning and went on our way. I remembered as I sat in the back of the car, I began talking to the Lord and the Spirit of the Lord started to speak to me about the person that we were going to meet. The Holy Spirit told me that it was a man that had cancer and that it runs in his family tree. So, I shared what the Holy Spirit said with the two ministers that were in the car with me. When we arrived at the train station, we were already fifteen minutes late. We repented for being late and apologized to the Lord. As we stood there, we began to search for this person that the Lord had showed us. We began to wonder if we missed him because we were late. After being there a while, watching train after train, we combed the area with our eyes looking to see if a man would walk towards us. We were there for about an hour until we decided to pray again and ask for instructions. But then the Holy Spirit instructed us that at 12 o'clock he would be there. While we were there waiting, one of the minister got a call that Pastor Zachery Tims had died. We were shocked. This was sad news; we were lost for words but we had to stay focus on what God sent us at the train station to do.

We got tired after standing for a while, so we sat down on a bench that no one occupied. While we sat there, we saw a man coming towards us! He was staggering, he stretched his hands out towards the minister and the minister shook his hand. This man was so drunk, you could smell the alcohol as if he had be washed in it. The spirit of the Lord told us that this was the man that we were looking for, and so we started to speak to him. We asked him his name and how he was doing, he was just mumbling words at times but he was able to respond. He began to tell us his story, and he pulled his shirt up so that we could see the Foley catheter on his stomach. He told us that he had cancer and that his mother had and sister had both succumbed to this dreaded disease. We started to minister to him but he was reluctant. He said, *"Where was God when my sister died? Why do I have cancer?"* He went through a lot so he had a lot of questions and needed answers. Some of his stories were quite inaudible, we could not hear them well because his speech was mingled in the alcohol on his breath. We tried to lead him into the sinner's prayer but he would not cooperated. We still prayed for him anyway. We told this sick man that God wants to heal him because he sent us there for him, but he still was not receptive. He was stone drunk, and he walked away from us. As he walked, we followed him, begging God to save him. We knew that God would get the glory out of his life! We were believing God for him, but he did not believe God for himself.

There are many people that go through numerous tragedies in their life. They asked questions like this sick man at the train station. **Where is God? Is there is a God?** I want to let you know that God is here right now! The omnipresent God is alive and he sees everything that you are going through. Proverbs 15: 3 says, "The eyes of the Lord are in every place, beholding the evil and the good." The book of Job is a perfect example of how God will allow bad things to happen for his glory. When bad things happened, we are so focused on the hurt and the pain, and the things that we lost. We get angry with God and at times, but in the situation there is a greater cause to every tragedy in our life. We may not understand it now, but we will get the revelation later. Sometimes your hurt and pain become your testimony to help someone else who is going through the same situation to get deliverance and healing. Your testimony will give someone the reassurance that they can survive what they are going through. They will begin to say," *If she went through THIS THING and make it OUT, then I can go through it too.*" In Job 23:10, the bible says, "*But he knoweth the way that I take: when he hath tried me, I shall come forth as gold*". *Without a test you don't have a testimony, trials come to make you stronger, what don't kill you, make you stronger! Some people went through situations where the tragedy birth the ministry in them.* "*And we know that all things work together for good to them who are the called according to his purpose.*"(Romans 8:28) in John 16:33, the bible encourages us by saying, "*These things I have spoken unto you, that in me ye might have peace.*" We must have tribulations in this world but we must be of good cheer. If the Lord overcame this world, we will overcome the world also.

Please allow me to testify: I was in church one night and I heard the Lord said to me," you are going to meet a school chancellor." I said ok Lord. The next day, we were at a dealership waiting for a car to be approved when I heard the Lord spoke to me. He said," I am sending you tomorrow morning to Fairfield Exit 14 in New Jersey and I will have someone there waiting to bless you." I asked for a pen and paper and wrote it down. Early the next morning, we met and was our way to New Jersey. When we got to Exit 14, we did not know what to do next so we stopped and parked for a few minutes. The driver of the car got impatient and drove off looking for a specific place where *he thought* the Lord would send us. Do you believe that sometimes when God give us an instruction or a part of an instruction, we will get impatient with him, especially if we have to wait on the next move? We may even start to think ahead of him and move when he did not tell us to move! In Proverbs 3:5 -6, we are encouraged to, trust in the Lord with all thine heart; and lean not unto thine own understanding. In all thy ways acknowledge him and he shall direct our paths.

Our directions or instructions must come from God. We did not ask for any more instructions when we reached Exit 14, and so we got lost for an hour and a half. We kept going around in circles, and all three of us in the car began to feel frustrated. This reminds me of the children of Israel went around in circles for forty years because of disobedience. We drove until the gas in the car got low and we had to replenish the tank. We had no money left, so we decided that we have to pray. We prayed and the Lord instructed us to go back to where we got off the exit. After the Lord spoke, I saw the front of the building in my spirit in an open vision. So we drove slowly back as the Lord instructed. I was looking for the building that the LORD showed me in the vision, the spirit of the Lord spoke to one of members of our team and gave her the name of the cross street. As we reached the cross street, I saw the building that the Holy Spirit flashed in my spirit. It was a church, I got out of the car and walked towards to the church. As we moved towards the door, I began to ask, *"Is anyone here?"* Then I heard the voice of a man says, "Come in!" It was an elderly man sitting around a desk with another man sitting at the side. I greeted them and introduce myself. I told him that I was from New York and the Lord sent us there. I told him there are three of us and he said, "Go get them!" so I went and got the rest of my team.

We began to tell him the story, he was very calm. He wasn't surprised either. He told us that he wasn't always at the church during the week but he felt he needed to be there that day. He mentioned that the other person with him was his longtime friend that he hasn't seen in a long time, so he called him that day to invite for lunch. My God! What a set up! God had a plan in motion. The Apostle did not speak much English, he spoke in Spanish but his friend spoke both English and Spanish. The Apostle which was the elderly, said "Let's pray in Spanish." As his friend interprets, the glory of the Lord filled the office. He had such a powerful anointing on his life. It was like he was transformed into someone else! All three of us knelt on our knees in surrender to the Lord. As he laid his hands and prophesied to each one of us, we felt an impartation upon us. I will never forget that moment God showed up and showed off like only he could! God works in mysterious ways. We just have to trust and obey. After the Apostle prayed for us, he took us in the sanctuary and we all prayed again, but then we had no money to return home. We did not say anything to him, but he blessed us with three hundred dollars. Glory to God!

I have had many experiences with God's goodness and mercy. God is the same yesterday, today, and forevermore. When I looked over my life I thought about my past, I realized that God has been keeping me throughout the years. When God has his hand upon you, he will keep you for his glory and his purpose. My walk with God has being a silent struggle. I know how to put on a face when I go to church but behind closed door, I was struggling with rejection. I needed someone to love me and my children but I found the answer in Jesus. Sometimes we may we say that we trust God, but at times, our faith is being tested and fear begin to hover us. Every day I wake up thanking God for his grace and his mercy that has kept me this far. It was prayer that kept me sane and is still preserving my soul. Even when I couldn't pray, I would be sleeping at nights and find myself waking up, speaking in tongues. The Holy Spirit was praying for me. In our weakness, he is made strong; Glory be to God! The bible says when the enemy comes in like a flood the spirit of the Lord will lift up a standard against him. People of God, I owe it all to Jesus. He has given me the strength to press through the flesh. Paul said, "I count not myself to have apprehended: but this one thing I do, forgetting those things which are behind, and reaching forth unto those things which are before, I press towards the mark for the prize of the high calling of God in Christ Jesus".

God will put us in situations where our faith will be tested. There will be tests at every level in your Christian walk. Sometimes God will bring you down to pull you up so that he can get the glory out of your life. When your back is against the wall, God will make a way of escape for you. I can testify that he did it for me over and over again. Trust God, he is my way maker and my 'head- lifter'. He is a God that never fails! Words cannot explain his goodness and his lovingkindness towards me. Paul says in Romans 7:18-21, "For I know that in me (that is, in my flesh,) dwelleth no good thing: for to will is present with me; but how to perform that which is good I find not. For the good that I would I do not: but the evil which I would not, that I do. Now if I do that I would not, it is no more I that do it, but sin that dwelled in me".

God will allow us to be in desperate situations where no one can help, but him. In John 11, when Lazarus was sick, they called Jesus to heal him but he did not show up until four days after he died. The Lord will show up when we are in a dead situation.

He showed up for Lazarus because he is the resurrection and the life. He showed up so that God will be glorified. The bible said he called Lazarus to come forth from the grave, and the dead man obeyed and got out of his dead situation, and came back to life, but he was still bound. There are believers out there that serve God but still don't believe in is resurrection power. They say it but when it is time for them to believe him in a dead situation, doubt messes with their mind. Some of you are still bound in your grave clothes, but Jesus wants to loose you. Have you ever been at a dead end in your life and you see no way out? You have tried everything but it seems like nothing is working for you. You have been searching for help but you are looking in the wrong places. Think about the lady with the issue of blood how she tried everything but nothing worked in her favor. She was determined to be delivered no matter the cost. The bible said she sought many physicians and depleted all that she had, but it did not help. But when she heard that JESUS was passing by, she never gave up. She was in a place of desperation, she was ready to be delivered and she was not waiting to be touched by Jesus. She wanted to touch him instead!

Are you in a place of desperation? Do you need something from the Lord? Have you reached a point in your life when your only choice is to try Jesus? You have done all that you could in your own strength and it is not working, well it's time to try Jesus. He is the "ingredient" that is missing from your life. The Lord is just waiting for us to place our situations in his hand.

He wants to resurrect the dead things and transform you into something better. Do not hold on to the things that only Jesus can change. Take your burdens to Jesus! I can assure you that he will turn it around for you. God is a Problem Solver, the good news is that he is able. There is nothing impossible for God! He can do exceedingly, abundantly, above all we can ask or think, he is bigger than our problems. May God be glorified in your life forever more, Amen.

Printed in the United States
by Baker & Taylor Publisher Services